# SoJourn

Volume 4, Number 1

A journal devoted to the history, culture, and geography of South Jersey

## SJCHC

South Jersey Culture & History Center

Summer 2019

*SoJourn* is a collaborative effort. Local historians contribute the articles; Stockton students—in this issue, the editing interns of spring 2019—edit the text, set the type, and design the layout; the directors of the South Jersey Culture & History Center at Stockton University oversee the publication.

**Editors**
Mariana Isabel Ramos Arias, Samantha Brown, Sviatlana Buslovich, Jessica Chamberlain, Katie Cushinotto, Kolette Deyo, Adira Fuller-Warren, Kyle Hovsepian, Samantha Hutnick, Ericka Naranjo, Marilyn Roman, Samantha Wyld.

**Supervising Editors**
Tom Kinsella and Paul W. Schopp

ISSN: 2474-6665
ISBN-13: 978-1-947889-95-8
A publication of the South Jersey Culture & History Center
at Stockton University
www.stockton.edu/sjchc/

Filler images, at the conclusion of articles, courtesy of the Paul W. Schopp Collection unless otherwise noted.

**To contact SJCHC write:**
SJCHC / School of Arts & Humanities
Stockton University
101 Vera King Farris Drive
Galloway, New Jersey
08205

**Email:**
Thomas.Kinsella@stockton.edu
Paul.Schopp@stockton.edu

## About this Issue of *SoJourn*

The deeper I dig into the history of South Jersey, the greater my admiration grows for the region. I am not native to the area, having arrived thirty years ago to teach at Stockton State College. I am not a historian by training; I am a member of Stockton's literature program. My areas of expertise are eighteenth-century English literature, medieval Irish literature, and English grammar. But the lure of South Jersey has captured my full attention. The eight southernmost counties of New Jersey are striking in the richness of their history and the diversity of their cultural development. The farmlands of Salem County are distinct from the Pinelands and, over time, developed different cultures with divergent customs and lifeways. The river counties of Salem, Gloucester, Camden, and Burlington are quite unlike the shore counties of Ocean, Atlantic, and Cape May. And the bay counties of Cape May (on its other shore), Cumberland, and Salem (on its bay side) are also distinctive. I don't mean to overstate the differences, which are often quite subtle. The region has long been bound by common ties woven through commerce, transportation, proximity, and political expedience. Still, South Jersey, first home to the Lenni Lenape, has a richly diverse history. Crossing through time, from the seventeenth century through the nineteenth, various immigrant groups have established communities here: the Dutch, Swedes, Finns, English, African Americans, Germans, Italians, and Jews. *SoJourn* attempts to record various facets of the cultural richness that derive from these communities and their history.

The articles in the current issue trace the coasts of South Jersey. Three describe places and events close to or along the Delaware River. Several more focus on places and events situated close to or directly on the Jersey coastline of Ocean and Atlantic counties. We remain indebted to our authors, local historians, and Stockton students for these excellent articles, and we encourage anyone with pertinent articles or stories to contact the *SoJourn* editors so that future issues will include your work.

Tom Kinsella

Director
South Jersey Culture & History Center
Stockton University

# MAP OF CONTENTS

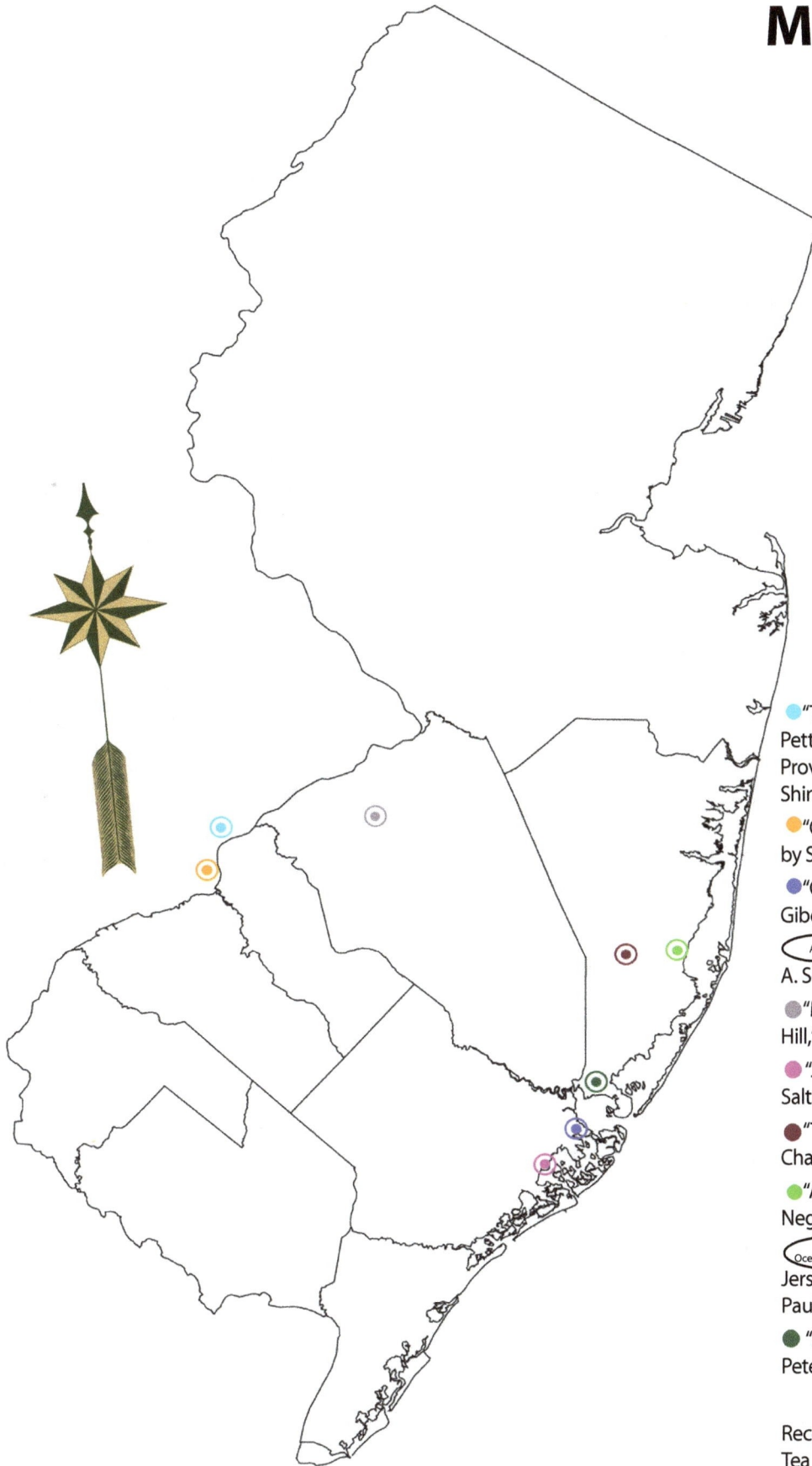

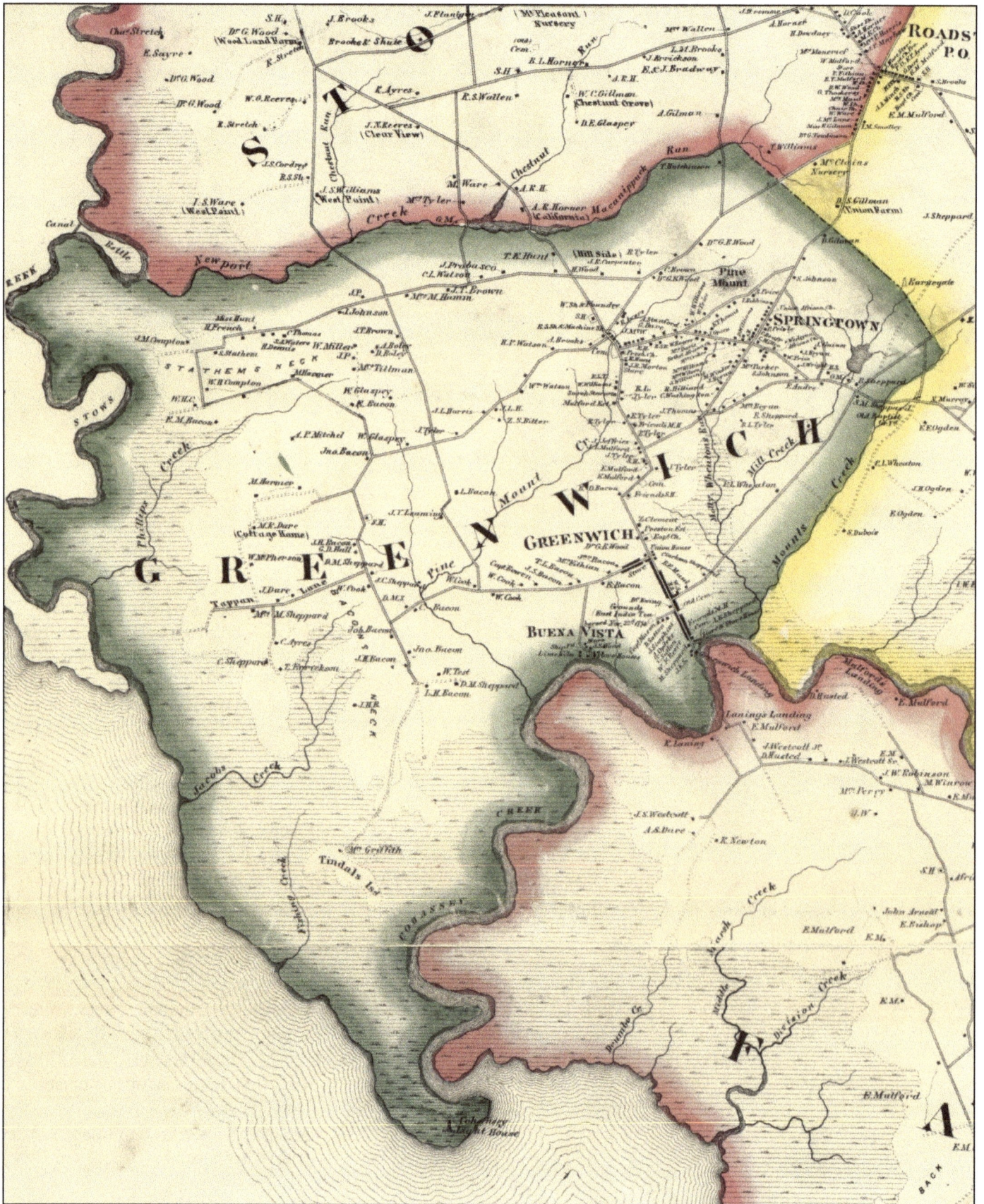

Detail of Greenwich Township from *Map of Cumberland Co., New Jersey: From Actual Surveys by S. N. & F. W. Beers, L. Blake & C. W. Warner* (Philadelphia: A. Pomeroy, 1862). Courtesy of the Library of Congress.

# The Great Island Lying Before Shackamaxon:
## Petty Island, Lenape-Colonist Relations, and Provincial Rivalries, 1678–1701

### Robert A. Shinn and Jean R. Soderlund

With significant progress made by 2019 in restoring Petty Island from an industrial site to a nature preserve that the New Jersey State Natural Lands Trust will own and manage, the island's location between Philadelphia and Camden offers a stark contrast to the surrounding metropolitan area. Despite substantial changes to the island since the seventeenth century, as engineers removed acreage from its west side to extend Philadelphia's exterior wharf line, the riverine place offers considerable insight into the perspectives and goals of Lenape Indians and European settlers as they vied to control events in the Delaware Valley. The island's early history exemplified the ways in which the Lenapes and colonists viewed the river and its lands. While the Delaware served as the region's central highway for the Indians and many Europeans increasingly after the founding of the Burlington colony in 1677 and Pennsylvania in 1681, the river became a political flashpoint as the provinces competed for regional control. The "greate Island lying before Shak[amaxon],"[1] as it was called, evolved during the quarter century from 1678 to 1701 from a site where Quaker immigrant Elizabeth Kinsey struck a deal to share the island with four Lenape sachems—who included the woman Ojroqua—to a source of conflict over resources and provincial squabbling between the West New Jersey Proprietors and William Penn.

The island underwent successive name changes after European arrival in the seventeenth century. Peter Lindeström, a Swedish engineer who surveyed the Delaware Valley in 1654–1655, recorded the island's Lenape name, Æquikonaska, on his map of New Sweden. The Europeans changed the name several times, to Shackamaxon Island, Fairman's Island, Treaty Island, and Petty (or, less properly, Petty's) Island, its current name, which appellation came from a later owner, Philadelphia merchant John Petty, who purchased it in 1732.[2]

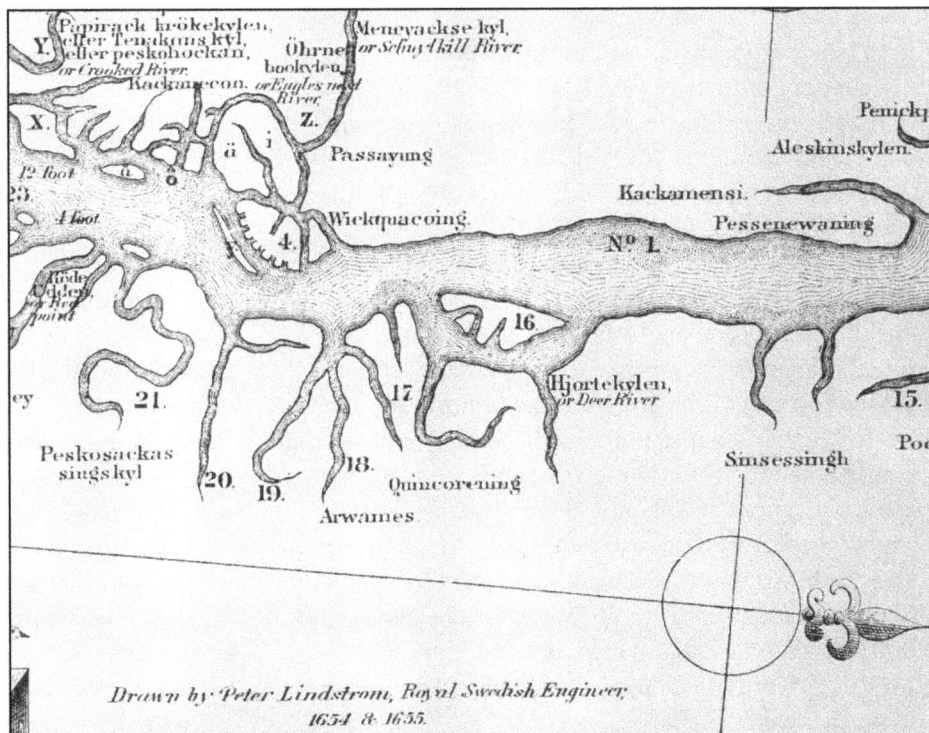

Figure 1. Detail from a map of *Nova Suecia, eller the Swenska Revier [now Delaware River] in India Occidentalis* created by Peter Lindestrom,1655, showing the island Æquikonaska (Petty Island) numbered "16."

Four seventeenth-century documents provide more evidence than is the norm about initial relations between Lenapes and colonists as they negotiated how to share land in the Delaware Valley. The documents include: the deed for Shackamaxon Island, dated July 12, 1678, from four Lenape sachems to Elizabeth Kinsey; a release of rights, dated June 10, 1698, to the island from Gunnar Rambo to Thomas Fairman, who had married Kinsey in 1680; and two confirmations of the 1678 deed from the Lenape woman Ojroqua, both probably dated July 4, 1698.[3] The 1678 deed and 1698 release, within the Quaker and Special Collections at Haverford College, have been known and published previously.[4] Our recent discovery of the two confirmations at the Camden County Historical Society has prompted new research in several areas, yielding further information about the Lenapes involved; the larger context of Lenape-European deeds and relations; the significance of the 1678 deed's content and its implementation; Fairman's efforts to retain control of the island; and the conflict generated between West New Jersey and Pennsylvania. The deed, release, and confirmations collectively provide unique insight into specific details about the bargain between Kinsey and the Lenapes, and their continuing relationship involving annual payments and confirmations. Also interesting is the fact that three women figured prominently in the 1678 negotiations as a grantor, grantee, and witness.

When Europeans landed in the seventeenth century, the Lenapes dominated the Delaware Valley in population and power. They resided in autonomous towns along creeks leading to the Delaware River and Bay in the region that became eastern Pennsylvania, West New Jersey, and northern Delaware and along the Atlantic seashore in Jersey. The Lenapes traveled frequently by canoe on rivers and creeks to conduct trade, hunt, fish, and gather food and other resources. While their population is uncertain prior to contracting European diseases, for which the Indians lacked immunity, in the mid-1630s the Lenapes numbered at least 7,500 and had recently defended their homeland successfully against the Susquehannocks of central Pennsylvania. As the Dutch, Swedes, and English established forts and small colonies, they brought successive epidemics of smallpox and other diseases. Still, in 1671, the Lenapes numbered 3,000, compared with 850 colonists, and retained the power to determine where settlers could take up land and participate in trade.[5]

Prior to 1675, few Europeans lived on the east bank of the Delaware in what became West New Jersey. The Dutch had initially entered the region for trade circa 1615, then established, in 1624, a short-lived colony on Burlington Island and, in 1626, built Fort Nassau, which functioned seasonally, where Gloucester City is located today. Before 1675, most colonists resided on the west bank between what are now New Castle and Philadelphia. They included Swedes, Finns, Germans, and Dutch who arrived beginning in 1638 as part of the New Sweden expedition; Dutch soldiers and settlers who came when New Netherland took control of the Swedish colony in 1655; and English soldiers and settlers who accompanied the forces of James, Duke of York, in their conquest of the Dutch colony in 1664. While some English, Swedes, and Finns established farmsteads on the east bank during the era when New Sweden maintained Fort Elfsborg near the present site of Salem from 1643 to 1651, it is unclear how long they remained. A few Dutch and French colonists moved to southwestern New Jersey in the late 1660s, purchasing land from the Indians. Written evidence of sustained Swedish and Finnish settlement in the region begins in 1668, when Lucas Peterson obtained a license from New Jersey Governor Philip Carteret and negotiated a deed with the Cohanseys in 1671. According to English records and Lenape deeds, Swedes and Finns first settled in present Gloucester County by 1673.[6]

The European population grew substantially in the Delaware Valley following a sequence of large land transfers originating in 1664 with King Charles II granting all of New Jersey to his brother, James, the Duke of York, who then granted the colony to Sir John Berkeley and Sir George Carteret. In 1674, Berkeley sold his half, which became West New Jersey, to Quaker John Fenwick in trust for another Quaker, Edward Byllynge, who then quarreled with Fenwick. Quakers William Penn, Gawen Lawrie, and Nicholas Lucas agreed to serve as trustees to resolve the dispute and establish a unified colony. Fenwick opposed their plan, demanding one-tenth of the proprietorship to start his own settlement. When Byllynge tried to give him the tenth in dispersed places across West New Jersey, Fenwick took his share in one location, which he called Salem, and sold 148,000 acres to circa 50 purchasers. When he arrived with his colonists in 1675, Fenwick promptly purchased territory from the local Lenapes—the Cohanseys—with whom he maintained good relations. Deeds of 1675 and 1676 specified that Fenwick, in return for cloth, rum, guns, and other trade goods, would receive land "Excepted allways . . . the Plantations in w^ch [the Cohanseys] now Inhabite."[7]

To respond to Fenwick's unilateral move, Byllynge's trustees, Penn, Lawrie, and Lucas, appointed a commission, in August 1676, led by London surgeon James Wasse, to negotiate with Fenwick concerning land title issues and to locate sites for new towns, the first of which would consist of four or five thousand acres with land twenty or thirty miles long about the town as liberties.[8] According to *A Mapp of Virginia Mary-land, New-Jarsey, New-York, & New England* by John Thornton and Robert Greene (Figure 2), the only remaining evidence of Wasse's work, he located one town, which he named Bethlem, at the Lenape site of Arawames (now Gloucester City); a second town at the Falls (now Trenton); and a third town, which he named Antioch Township, on land he had purchased from Fenwick.[9]

In 1677, when the ship KENT arrived with 230 settlers to establish the second West New Jersey colony after Fenwick, they found it necessary to deviate from Wasse's plan. Arriving in late summer, they received shelter and food from the Lenapes and from the Swedes and Finns residing in a settlement centered on Raccoon Creek. The Swedes and Finns also helped the new colonists to obtain deeds from the Lenapes for three large areas along the east bank of the Delaware: from Oldmans to Big Timber creeks, between Big Timber and Rancocas creeks, and from Rancocas Creek to Assunpink Creek. At first, the Quakers from Yorkshire traveled to the Falls for settlement, as Wasse had designated, while those from London began settling at Wasse's proposed town of Bethlem. When the Yorkshire Quakers realized how far they would be settling away from the Londoners, they proposed "if they would agree to fix by them, they would join in settling a town, and that they [the Londoners] should have the largest share, in consideration that they (the Yorkshire commissioners) had the best land in the woods: Being few, and the Indians numerous, they [the Londoners] agreed to it."[10] Within a month of arriving, the London settlers abandoned Bethlem at Arawames and most of the Yorkshire Quakers left the Falls, to create the compromise settlement of Burlington. When the winter of 1677–78 delayed construction, they built wigwams like the Lenapes' and depended upon the Indians for corn, vegetables, venison, fish, and fowl. The colonists brought smallpox that unfortunately killed many Lenapes—as had earlier epidemics initiated with the Swedes, Dutch, and English.[11]

Despite this disease, Lenapes retained considerable power in West Jersey as the European population remained quite small and settlements dispersed. The Lenapes, with additional

Figure 2. Detail from *A mapp of Virginia Mary-land, New-Jarsey, New-York, & New England* by John Thornton and Robert Greene dated 1673.

mortality by 1700, lost their numerical superiority to the colonists, though they continued to leverage influence through personal relationships and, when necessary, threats of violence. An estimated 1,760 Friends settled in the colony by 1682, but after that date most immigrants to the Delaware Valley settled in Pennsylvania, which, by 1700, held nearly 18,000 Europeans, compared with approximately 3,500 settlers in West Jersey. As colonists arrived and spread out from Trenton south to Cape May, they set up autonomous communities governed by county courts. Though Byllynge and his colleagues had founded Burlington as West New Jersey's capital, centralized government proved impossible due to the dispersed settlements and a power vacuum developed among the elites resulting from struggles over land, leadership, and the English government's efforts to repeal the proprietorship.[12]

In 1678, four Lenapes, including one woman, placed their marks on a deed granting an unmarried young Quaker woman, Elizabeth Kinsey (c. 1660–1720), rights to use the "greate Island lying before Shak[amaxon]" in the Delaware River.

The daughter of John and Mary Kinsey of Much Haddam, Hertfordshire, England, Elizabeth had immigrated in 1677 with her father, who was an associate of Quaker founder George Fox and, like Fox and thousands of other Friends, endured persecution for his faith. John Kinsey, a maltster and self-described gentleman of some estate, on March 1 and 2, 1677, purchased one proprietary (a right to a hundredth share of the Province of West New Jersey) for £350 from Edward Byllynge through his trustees. Kinsey sold two-thirds of his proprietary before leaving England, and his son, John, who arrived in Burlington in 1678, sold the remaining one-third in 1681.[13] John Sr. died on October 11, 1677, shortly after his arrival on the ship GREYHOUND at Wicaco, near Old Swedes Church (in present Philadelphia), leaving Elizabeth to settle his affairs. Before passing away, he had agreed to purchase a three-hundred acre plantation at Shackamaxon from the Swedish interpreter and trader, Lasse Cock and his wife Martha, a deal Elizabeth completed in March 1678.[14]

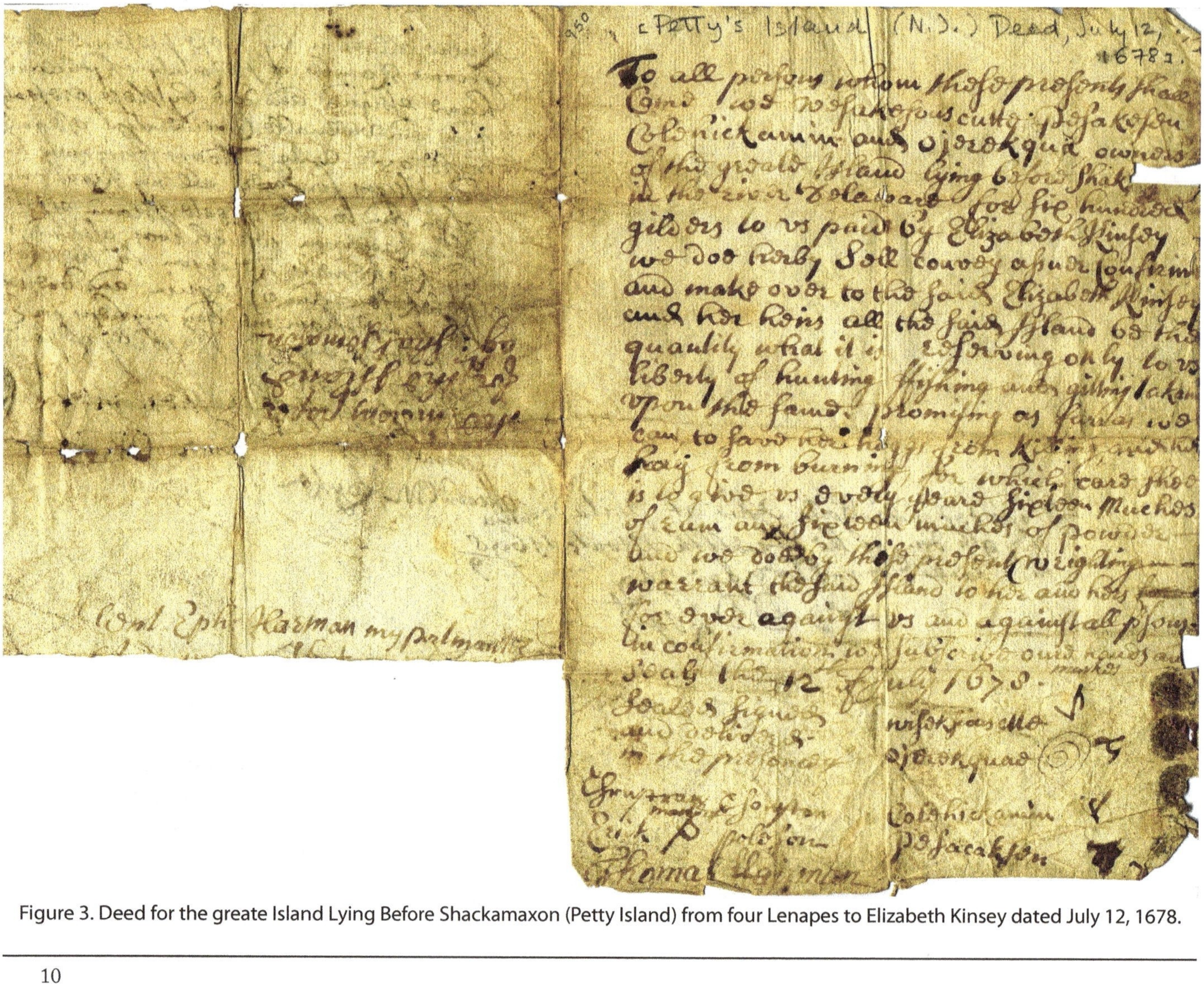

Figure 3. Deed for the greate Island Lying Before Shackamaxon (Petty Island) from four Lenapes to Elizabeth Kinsey dated July 12, 1678.

Figure 4. Detail from *A Map of the Improved Part of the Province of Pennsilvania in America, begun in 1681* by Thomas Holmes, Surveyor General, showing the location of Shackamaxon relative to "the great Island" (Petty Island) and Philadelphia and the names of property owners and original purchasers from William Penn.

Four months later, in July 1678, Elizabeth Kinsey also acquired Shackamaxon Island in a deed that exemplified the good relations that the Lenapes, Swedes, and Finns had established prior to Quaker settlement and that continued under West New Jersey and William Penn. The deed is also unique and enlightening in suggesting how women could make agreements and foster relationships across the cultural divide between colonists and Lenapes. More clearly than many contemporaneous deeds, the 1678 compact with Elizabeth Kinsey spelled out the Lenapes' expectation that they would retain rights to use the island rather than transfer full ownership. Since the Dutch, Swedes, and English first came to the Delaware Valley in the early seventeenth century, Lenapes had welcomed them to build trading posts and small settlements in return for annual payments and commercial ties. Trouble could erupt when Europeans misunderstood the limits of the Lenape grants or willfully claimed more land than the Lenapes intended. The Indians also reclaimed the land if the Europeans failed to use it at all. While we know this from incidents such as Lenape killings of colonists and resale of land that remained unoccupied following its initial sale—as well as references to continuing Lenape rights in some other deeds—the 1678 Kinsey document specified the terms of conveyance better than most.[15]

## DEED FOR SHACKAMAXON ISLAND FROM LENAPES TO ELIZABETH KINSEY JULY 12, 1678[16]

To all persons whom these presents shall Come we Wesakesous cutte Pesakesen Colehickamin and Ojerekqua owners of the greate Island lying before Shak[amaxon][17] in the river Delaware for six hundred gilders to us paid by Elizabeth Kinsey we doe herby Sell convey assuer Confirm and make over to the said Elizabeth Kinsey and her heirs all the said Island be the quantity what it is reserving only to us liberty of hunting Fishing and gitting takah[o] upon the same, promising as farr as we can to save her hoggs from Killing, and her hay from burning, for which care shee is to give us every yeare sixteen Muches of rum and sixteen muches of powder[18]—and we doe by these[19] present wrighting—warrant the said Island to her and hers for ever against us and against all p'rsons. in confirmation we subscribe oure hands an[d] seals the 12th of July 1678.

| | |
|---|---|
| Sealed Signed | Wiseksious ctte [mark] |
| and deliverd | Ojerekquae [spiral & other mark] |
| in the presence of | |
| Prudence Clayton | Colehickamin [mark] |
| mark of | |
| Erick P poleson | Pesacakson [mark] |
| Thomas Fairman | |

According to the deed, the Lenapes would retain the right to hunt, fish, and dig edible plants (tuckahoe) on the island in exchange for promising to protect Kinsey's hogs from being killed "and her hay from burning." In return, Kinsey paid six hundred guilders sewant (approximately £15 sterling) and annual payments of rum and gunpowder. Though the document indicates "gilders," it is clear that the deal was for guilders sewant, a book currency commonly used in the Delaware Valley in the 1670s and early 1680s. With a value of 40 guilders sewant (often abbreviated in accounts as "g.s.") to the English £ sterling and 4 g.s. to the Holland guilder, the amount Kinsey paid for rights to Shackamaxon Island is more in line with, though still higher than, payments the West New Jersey colonists paid for other parcels than if she paid in Holland guilders. The Dutch, Swedish, and English colonists developed this book currency based on the value of wampum due to the lack of European coin. Similar to checks or credit cards today, the Lenape sachems could use Kinsey's note to purchase goods in New Castle or New York, or from local traders.[20]

Kinsey subsequently changed the annual payments from rum and gunpowder to one matchcoat, or woolen Indian garment, per year. Many of the early land transactions in West New Jersey included payments of rum, as did the first deed that Penn's agent, William Markham, negotiated with the Lenapes in Pennsylvania in 1682. Like the Dutch and Duke of York's governments before them, both Pennsylvania and West New Jersey prohibited colonists from selling rum and other alcohol to the Lenapes. The prohibition met with only limited success, as Europeans and Indians often ignored the laws. Also similar to the ban of the Duke of York's government on small quantities (but not those of more than two gallons), alcohol remained an important trade item in West New Jersey, with gallons of rum and beer included in deeds negotiated by representatives of proprietors Daniel Coxe and the West New Jersey Society in 1688 and 1693.[21] The position of Friends of Philadelphia Yearly

Meeting, who disciplined those members who sold alcohol to the Lenapes, likely influenced Elizabeth Kinsey to change the annual payment to a matchcoat. Indeed, the first policy statement, dated 1691, of the women's Philadelphia Yearly Meeting, which met alternately in Burlington and Philadelphia, directed members to follow "friends order as to the Indians that they should not give them any Strong Liquor to their hurt." Kinsey, like other Quakers, knew that Lenape sachems blamed alcohol—and the colonists who sold it—for deaths of "seven Score of our People . . . since the time it was first sold us."[22]

Close study of the 1678 deed, Rambo's 1698 release, Ojroqua's confirmations, and other contemporaneous evidence provides considerable information about the Lenapes with whom early Delaware Valley colonists negotiated and the nature of European-Indian relations. Despite differences in the ways colonists heard and recorded the sachems' names, we can determine with reasonable certainty that the four Lenapes who signed the 1678 deed to Elizabeth Kinsey had broad responsibilities in representing their communities and that their authority as sachems went well beyond negotiations for Shackamaxon Island. Ojroqua's 1698 confirmations indicate that she had signed the 1678 deed with her "brothers," which may have referred to close kinship or a more general relationship among sachems. As the Lenapes lost population and land during the seventeenth century, communities and families relocated and merged to consolidate their political, social, and economic power.

Of the four Lenape grantors who signed the 1678 deed for Shackamaxon Island, the life of Wassackarous (Wiseksious ctte on the 1678 deed, Wesekascutte on the 1698 Rambo release) is best documented.[23] Wassackarous signed deeds circa 1674 with other sachems in eastern Monmouth County, then moved south where, in May 1675, he was one of a delegation who met with Governor Edmund Andros at New Castle and, in 1675–1676, with the Cohanseys, signed land conveyances to John Fenwick and other settlers.[24] Wassackarous also later signed (recorded as Weskeakitt) the 1677 deed for the land from the Rancocas to Assunpink Creek, and (as Westkikett and Seketarius) signed several deeds in 1682 and 1683 to William Penn. While most Lenape sachems negotiated deeds for their specific territory, Wassackarous took a more far-reaching responsibility, perhaps because his family networks spanned many Lenape communities. It is also possible, like Lasse Cock and other Swedes and Finns who could speak Lenape, Wassackarous knew English and thus attended conferences with each new wave of English colonists in the 1670s and 1680s until his death around 1684. The fact that he actually signed many of these deeds as a grantor, rather than as

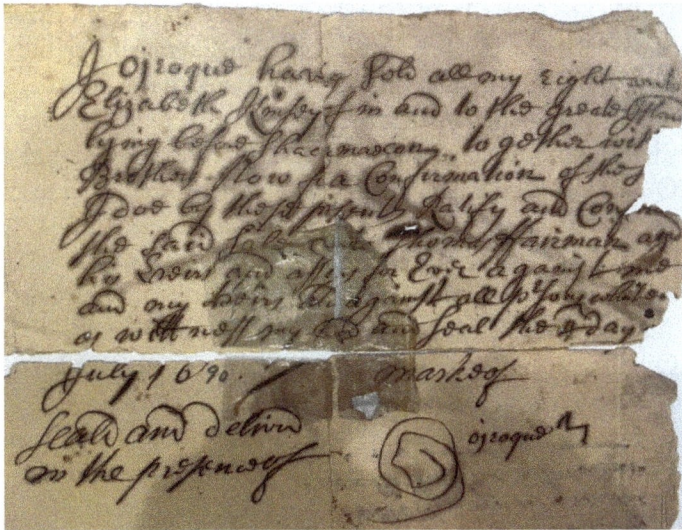

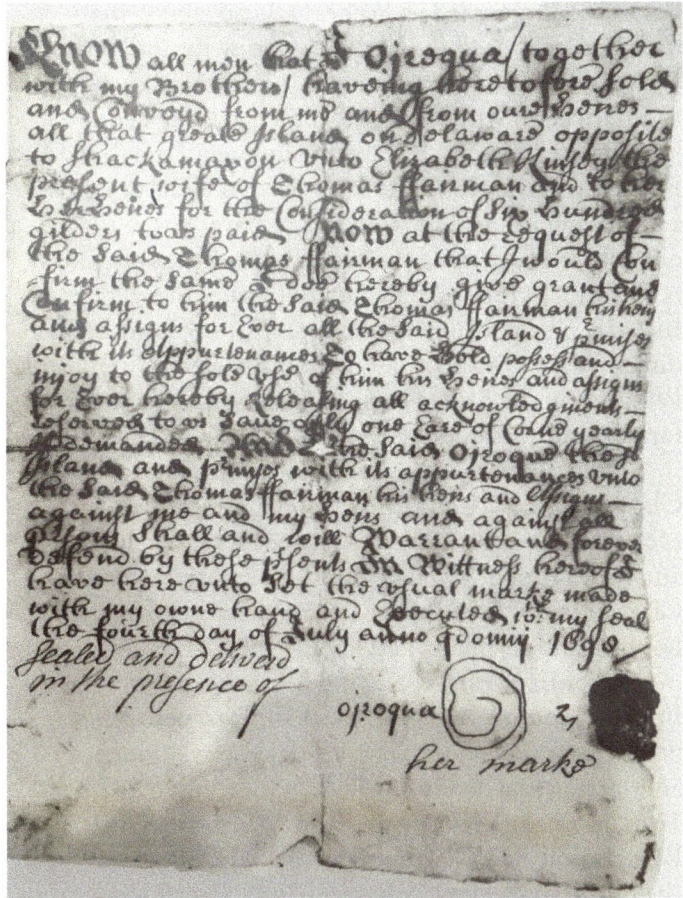

Figure 5. (Left) Ojroqua Draft Confirmation to Thomas Fairman July 4, 16[98]. Figure 6. (Right) Ojroqua Draft Confirmation (Second Version) to Thomas Fairman July 4, 1698.

a witness, suggests that he had family ties to the land or was accorded responsibility by Lenapes who held the territory in question.[25]

The second signer of the 1678 deed was Ojroqua (also spelled Ojerekqua, Ojerekquae, Ojrequia, Ojrequa, and Ojroque in these documents), who we learn from the 1698 confirmation was a woman when the European scribe indicated "her marke" of a spiral and what resembles bird's wings. Unlike some Lenape sachems, whose marks varied from one deed to another, Ojroqua used the same marks on these three documents. Her use of the spiral is unique in the lower Delaware Valley, though the symbol appears frequently in Native American culture. Ojroqua perhaps highlighted the significance for Lenapes of wampum, made from spiral-shaped shells.

Like Wassackarous, though to a lesser degree as far as we know, the sachem Ojroqua was involved in other diplomacy with Europeans, including the September 23, 1670, meeting (recorded as Oyagrakun) in West New Jersey to avoid further conflict arising from Lenape murders of Europeans who had encroached on their land. It is also likely, given her status and residence, that Ojroqua was one of the sachems who signed the September 27, 1677, deed for the land between Oldmans and Big Timber creeks.[26] Identifying her as a woman adds new evidence about the role of Lenape women in diplomatic encounters with Europeans in the seventeenth century. Male European colonizers, who controlled the written narrative, provided only glimpses of women's stature in Lenape matrilineal society in which they held significant political, social, and economic power. While European men were culturally inclined to deal with male Lenape sachems they some-

times called "kings," Lenape women served as kinship leaders, raised and controlled the distribution of crops, and produced wampum, among other duties. Prior to discovering Ojroqua's gender in the confirmation, we knew that two Lenape women—Notike and Necosshehesco—signed deeds for land near what are now New Castle, Delaware, and Salem, New Jersey, but, in each case, the European scribe suggested the woman participated as the mother of an underage son. With the 1678 deed for Shackamaxon Island and Ojroqua's confirmations, we see a female Lenape sachem who had taken part in prior conferences and, with the Fairmans, maintained a subsequent twenty-year relationship.[27]

Colehickamin and Pesacakson had also served as representatives to European officials, with Colehickamin (recorded as Quequirimen) and perhaps Pesacakson (recorded as Pemenacken) attending the September 23, 1670, conference. Colehickamin witnessed several deeds, including the 1682 grant to William Penn for lower Bucks County (recorded as Kowyockhicken) and the 1684 deed for Pennsauken, West New Jersey, to John Roberts et al. (recorded as Queieckolen). Colehickamin remained active as late as April 15, 1693, when (recorded as Callouque-hickon) he received compensation from Gloucester County Court for killing a panther.

Pesacakson (recorded as Pecheatus) had signed the October 1677 deed to West New Jersey for the territory between Rancocas and Assunpink creeks and (recorded as Piserickem) witnessed two 1683 deeds for Penn.[28]

For the Lenapes, Elizabeth Kinsey, and the three European witnesses to the 1678 deed, the Delaware River created opportunity and a means of travel rather than an obstacle. None seemed limited by thoughts of provincial boundaries as they operated on both sides of the river. In 1678, no colonial laws prevented Kinsey from dealing directly with Wassackarous, Ojroqua, Colehickamin, and Pesacakson; she gained their support against competitors for the land with the bargain they struck.

The three witnesses to the 1678 deed, Prudence Clayton, Eric Pålsson Mullica, and Thomas Fairman, each brought experience and perspectives to help the ambitious young woman expand her estate. Prudence Clayton had arrived in West New Jersey in 1677 with her husband, William, and family. They settled in Burlington for two years, where she took a leading role in the Friends Monthly Meeting, to which Elizabeth Kinsey belonged at that time. Clayton's daughters, Prudence and Honor, married in Burlington meeting in 1678 and 1679, just before Kinsey wed Thomas Fairman in 1680. By that time, the Clayton family had moved across the river to Marcus Hook, where, in 1681, Penn's Deputy, Governor William Markham, appointed both William Clayton and Fairman to his nine-man council.[29] The witness whose name is recorded on the 1678 deed as Erick Poleson (he signed with the mark P) was actually Eric Pålsson Mullica, who had emigrated from Sweden in 1654 with his father, Pål Jönsson, a Finn, and mother, Margaret. By 1678, Mullica lived with his wife and children at Tacony, just north of Shackamaxon. Later, in the 1690s, the family moved to Little Egg Harbor, New Jersey, on what became known as the Mullica River.[30]

The third witness was Thomas Fairman (c. 1650–1714), whom Elizabeth married on December 24, 1680, at the home of John Woolston in Burlington under the care of Burlington Monthly Meeting. Elizabeth and Thomas had much in common: they were from the same area of England (Hertfordshire), and born to Quaker families who likely traveled in the same circles in England before emigrating to America.[31] Thomas had arrived in Burlington before the Kinseys, learned to speak what was probably a trade version of the Lenape language and, similar to the Claytons, but unlike most West New Jersey immigrants, began purchasing land on the west side of the Delaware River. In 1679, Fairman took up 260 acres at Bensalem, Neshaminy Creek, and, on June 8, 1680, obtained a grant from the Upland Court for 200 more.[32]

At age 18 in 1678, Elizabeth Kinsey completed two real estate transactions: one for the Shackamaxon plantation with the Swedish trader Lasse Cock that her father had initiated; and the second with Lenape sachems for the rights to Shackamaxon Island. Like the 20-year-old Quaker woman Elizabeth Haddon who immigrated to West New Jersey in 1701 to manage her father's property, Kinsey used her feme sole status under English common law to make contracts and enlarge her holdings. Also similar to Haddon, Kinsey functioned within a Quaker community that offered support for her goals. The presence of Quaker leader Prudence Clayton as a witness to the 1678 deed reflects a kind of *in loco parentis* assistance from Quaker women for the tenacious teenager administering her part of her father's estate.[33]

The larger Burlington Quaker community also bolstered Kinsey's position on two occasions when individuals slandered her, perhaps thinking her both vulnerable and threatening as a strong, propertied woman.[34] When Samuel Cole accused her of some unnamed offense, Kinsey sued him for "Slander" at the June 1680 session of Burlington Court.[35] No record exists of further proceedings. Following her marriage to Thomas Fairman, Elizabeth became a feme covert under English common law, yielding to her husband her rights to control property and make contracts. She remained forthright, however, defending herself and Thomas in a letter to Burlington Monthly Meeting, undated but probably written during the early 1680s. She responded powerfully to rumors that she and her husband had committed fornication before marriage and neglected meetings (though the Friends met in their home!), and that she drank liquor excessively while pregnant and committed other unspecified sins. She apparently convinced the meeting that these "busie bodie & prejudiced persons" had made false reports "after the worst manner." She concluded respectfully that "having given in my Testemony being the naked Truth from the simplicity of my heart shall leave the Issue thereof to the Lord & the Judgment of friends." No evidence exists that the rumors about Elizabeth Fairman (and Thomas) were valid, as Burlington Monthly Meeting did not record any further action.[36]

After their marriage, the Fairmans did not reside long at Shackamaxon before welcoming a continuous flood of visitors and boarders who, soon after Penn received his charter in March 1681, made the Fairman home the first capital of Pennsylvania. By October 1681, the Fairmans boarded Markham and Penn's land commissioner, William Haige, and, by August 1682, provided accommodations to Captain Thomas Holme, the first Surveyor General of Pennsylvania, and his family and friends. In early 1683, a few months after Penn arrived in Pennsylvania, they rented him their home as his seat of government and to accommodate his large entourage. The Fairmans relocated temporarily to Tacony until Penn moved out.[37]

Thomas Fairman served Markham and the Pennsylvania proprietor in many ways, including in 1681, by serving as clerk to the Council and as a justice of the Upland court. In the fall of that year, he took soundings up and down the Delaware River at Markham's direction, seeking a suitable location for the future port city of Philadelphia. Once Markham and Haige settled on the land called Wicaco, belonging to the Swanson family, Markham appointed Fairman to negotiate its purchase. Fairman did much of the colony's survey work before the arrival of Thomas Holme and continued to survey land for William Penn as the Deputy Surveyor General, primarily in the area of today's Montgomery and Bucks counties. Fairman also surveyed and acquired land for his brother and the London Land Company. He later held the office of Pennsylvania Surveyor General after the death of Edward Penington in 1702.[38]

Shackamaxon (then Fairman's) Island remained an important part of the Fairmans' holdings, as it provided reeds and hay for their farm animals at their Pennsylvania Shackamaxon plantation and, if the original island deed accurately reflected Elizabeth's intentions, on the island itself. With their marriage, Thomas obtained under English common law Elizabeth's rights to both the Shackamaxon plantation and the island, for which,

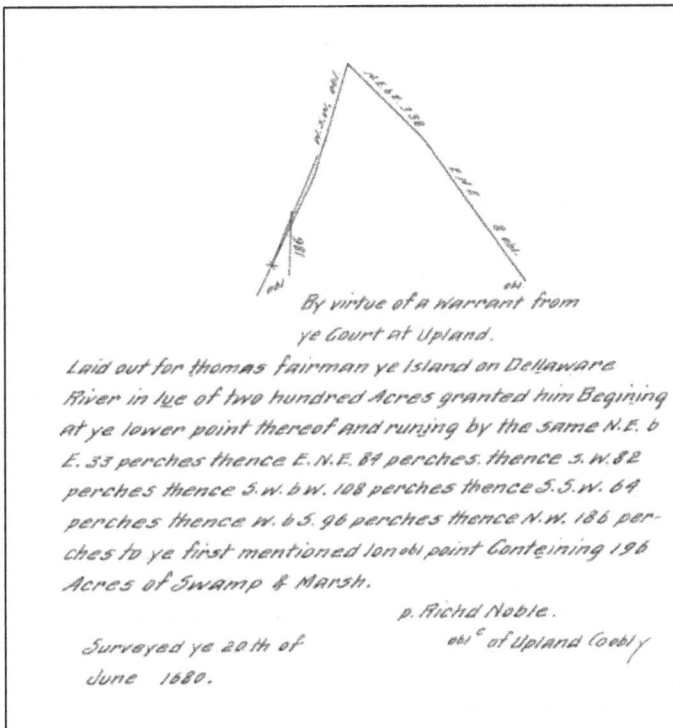

Figure 7. Land survey of "ye Island on Dellaware River" (Petty Island) by Richard Noble laid out for Thomas Fairman dated June 20, 1680, by virtue of a warrant from the Court at Upland.

in July 1680, anticipating their marriage, he submitted a survey of the island to the Upland Court pursuant to a previously issued warrant. (See Figure 7.) The survey notes that the island area surveyed was 198 acres and was "in lue [lieu] of two hundred Acres granted him."[39] As with other land conveyances in the early Delaware Valley, the Fairmans sought both a deed from the Lenapes and a patent of ownership from the colonial government.

Despite the 1678 Lenape deed and their submission of the survey in 1680, the Fairmans faced a series of challenges to their ownership of the island from both the West Jersey Proprietors and William Penn. Their early assistance to Penn and Thomas's continuing work as a surveyor probably helped them to prevail. In arguing their case, they emphasized their ongoing relationship with the Lenapes, especially Ojroqua, who provided the strongest evidence they possessed. Though Penn and some of his officials sometimes criticized Fairman's surveying practice, his relationship and services to the Pennsylvania proprietor were important factors in helping him to retain the island. No proceedings before the Upland Court confirmed their ownership pursuant to Fairman's July 1680 island survey similar to the certification that Lasse Cock gave to Elizabeth for the Shackamaxon plantation. Also absent are records indicating that the Fairmans ever paid quitrents or taxes on the island to either the Pennsylvania or West New Jersey proprietors before 1700.

According to Thomas Fairman, however, he and Elizabeth had retained their rights to Fairman's Island by honoring their commitment to the Lenapes: by paying the six hundred guilders sewant in 1678 and "a Matchcote every yeare." In 1698, they took advantage of that continuing relationship by obtaining a deed confirmation from Ojroqua, certifying that she and her "Brothers" had conveyed use rights to Elizabeth Kinsey twenty years before. The Fairmans perhaps sought these confirmations from Ojroqua to replace documents lost in the May 21, 1698, fire at the house of John Reading, clerk of the Council of West New Jersey Proprietors.[40] Even so, the reason for two drafts of the confirmation is unclear, but apparently someone decided that the shorter document needed more detail. The longer confirmation extinguished the rights to fishing, hunting, and gathering tuckahoe that the 1678 deed reserved for the Lenapes, and granted Fairman the right "To have Hold possess and injoy to the sole use of him his heires and assigns for Ever." It also released the Fairmans of all payments due to the Lenapes "save only one Eare of Corne yearly if demanded." Now twenty years after the original agreement, with the expansion of European colonization on both sides of the river, Ojroqua yielded full ownership of the island.

## OJROQUA DRAFT CONFIRMATION TO THOMAS FAIRMAN JULY 4, 16[98][41]

I Ojroque having sold all my right unto Elizabeth Kinsey of in and to the greate Island lying before Shacamaxon, together wit[h my] Brothers. Now [for?] a Confirmation of the [torn] I doe by these presents Ratify and Confirm the said sale unto Thomas Fairman and his heirs and ass[ig]ns for Ever against me and my heirs and against all p^rsons whatever as wittness my hand and seal the 4 day [of] July 16[98].[42]

Seald and deliverd                  marke of
in the presence of              [spiral] ojroque [mark]


## OJROQUA DRAFT CONFIRMATION TO THOMAS FAIRMAN JULY 4, 1698[43]

Know all men that I Ojrequa (together with my Brothers) haveing heretofore sold and Conveyd from me and from oure heires all that greate Island on delaware opposite to Shackamaxon unto Elizabeth Kinsey the present wife of Thomas Fairman and to her her heires for the Consideration of six hundred gilders to us paid Now at the request of the said Thomas Fairman that I would Confirm the same I doe hereby give grant and Confirm to him the said Thomas Fairman his heirs and assigns for Ever all the said Island & p^rmises with its Appurtenances To have Hold possess and injoy to the sole use of him his heires and assigns for Ever hereby Releasing all acknowledgments reserved to us save only one Eare of Corne yearly if demanded. And I the said Ojroque the s^d Island and p^rmises with its appurtenances unto the said Thomas Fairman his heirs and Assigns against me and my heirs and against all prsons shall and will Warrant and forever defend by these p^rsents In Wittness hereof I have here unto set the usual marke made with my owne hand and Executed w^th my seal the fourth day of July anno Domini 1698

Sealed and deliverd
in the presence of              ojroqua [spiral] [mark]
                                her marke

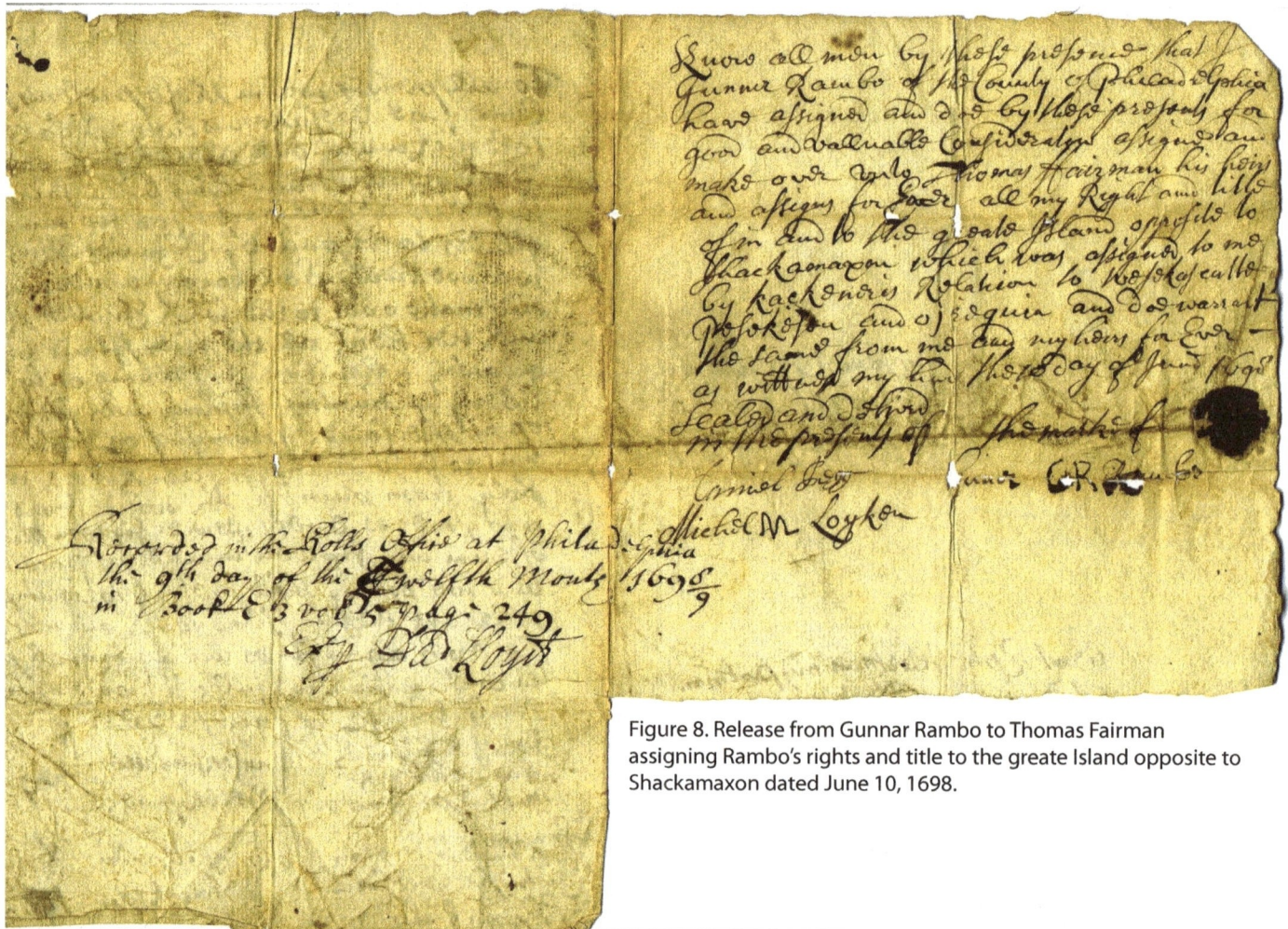

Figure 8. Release from Gunnar Rambo to Thomas Fairman assigning Rambo's rights and title to the greate Island opposite to Shackamaxon dated June 10, 1698.

On February 9, 1699, Fairman entered Elizabeth's original deed in the Rolls Office at Philadelphia with a release dated June 10, 1698, from neighbor Gunnar Rambo, one of the early and influential Swedes on the Delaware who served in the Pennsylvania Assembly (Figure 8). The release stated that for an undisclosed "good and valluable Consideration," Rambo was assigning and making over to Thomas Fairman and his heirs all his "Right and title of in and to the greate Island opposite to Shackamaxon," which "Kackeneris Relation to Wesekascutte Pesekesen and ojrequia" assigned to him.[44] The identity of Kackeneris and why he apparently transferred rights to the island to Rambo alone—and whether he did this before or after the 1678 deed to Kinsey—are unclear. He could have been Colehickamin because it is strange that his name is omitted from the release. The name Katamas/Catemus appears on other deeds not signed by Colehickamin, including the 1677 conveyance for the territory from Rancocas to Big Timber creeks and as a witness to three deeds to William Penn in 1683.[45] While "buyer beware" was not a frequent problem associated with Lenape conveyances, the possible grant of the same land to two different individuals or groups was sufficiently real and known to William Penn that he warned his commissioners in 1681 that while they should be "tender of offending the Indians," they should also "From time to time in my Name and for my use buy land of them, where any justly pretend, for they will sell one anothers, if you be not Carefull." In most cases, when Lenapes conveyed rights to a second purchaser, the first buyer had not taken up the land and/or made annual payments.[46]

### RELEASE FROM GUNNAR RAMBO TO THOMAS FAIRMAN FOR FAIRMAN'S ISLAND[47]

> Know all men by these presence that I Gunner Rambo of the County of Philadelphia have assigned and doe by these presents for good and valluable Consideration assigne and make over unto Thomas Fairman his heirs and assigns for Ever all my Right and title of in and to the greate Island opposite to Shackamaxon which was assigned to me by Kackeneris Relation to Wesekascutte Pesekesen and ojrequia and doe warrant the same from me and my heirs for Ever as wittnes my hand the 10 day of June 1698
> Sealed and delivrd
> in the presents of    The marke of
> Daniel Pegg     Guner GR Rambo
> Michel M Loyken

Fairman had good reason to validate the rights to the island that his wife had obtained from the Lenapes twenty years before. In a letter to Penn dated August 7, 1700, Fairman complained that Penn's secretary of the colony, James Logan, had issued permits to others to cut reeds on the island "without Limetation." Fairman wrote that he had previously tolerated some of his neighbors cutting reeds after Fairman had harvested enough for himself until Penn was "better Satisfyed of my right theire," but this new practice of allowing unlimited cutting left him with barely enough for two cows. Worse, Fairman wrote, Logan had imprudently discussed and questioned Fairman's rights to the island with those seeking permits. Fairman's letter advised Penn that in his absence "I use to thinke I wanted not so much a Title to the place as the Proprietors Protection from the Rabble & Jersey men." He said that Joseph Cooper of West Jersey had told others that "he would never aske Governour Penn leave to Cutt on any of the Islands For saies he the Proprietors in Burlington have lately asserted theire right to the Island and sent to them to Cutt."[48]

In fact, on June 25, 1700, the Council of West Jersey Proprietors in Burlington discussed their dispute with Pennsylvania over ownership of an island in the Delaware because West Jersey inhabitants were prevented from cutting the reeds. The Council instructed Governor Andrew Hamilton, Samuel Jennings, and Thomas Thackera to meet with Penn to determine the basis of his claim for the island. Hamilton probably conferred with Penn, as they were allies against efforts to cede the proprietary governments of East and West Jersey to the Crown, with Hamilton apparently agreeing that Penn should have the island.[49]

This claim of the Council in Burlington was not new, for Penn and the West New Jersey government had earlier wrangled over title to the Delaware islands. In June 1683, Penn instructed his commissioners concerning these boundary negotiations to "insist upon my Titul to the River, Soyl & Islands thereof. . . . Remember the Argument, They are bounded westward by the River Delaware, then they cannot go beyond low Water Mark for Land; They have the Liberty of the River but not the Propriety." The West New Jersey Assembly responded on September 8, 1683, by appointing representatives to treat with Penn. The issue remained unresolved and, in May 1691, Robert Turner wrote Penn "wee desire to Know how wee shall Justifye the lettinge of the Reed Islands from the clame of west Jersy, that wee may act saffly, for wee are unanimuse."[50] In his August 1700 letter to Penn, Fairman pointed out that he and Elizabeth "have been out of oure money I thinke Now Twenty three years 600 Guilders besids a Matchcote

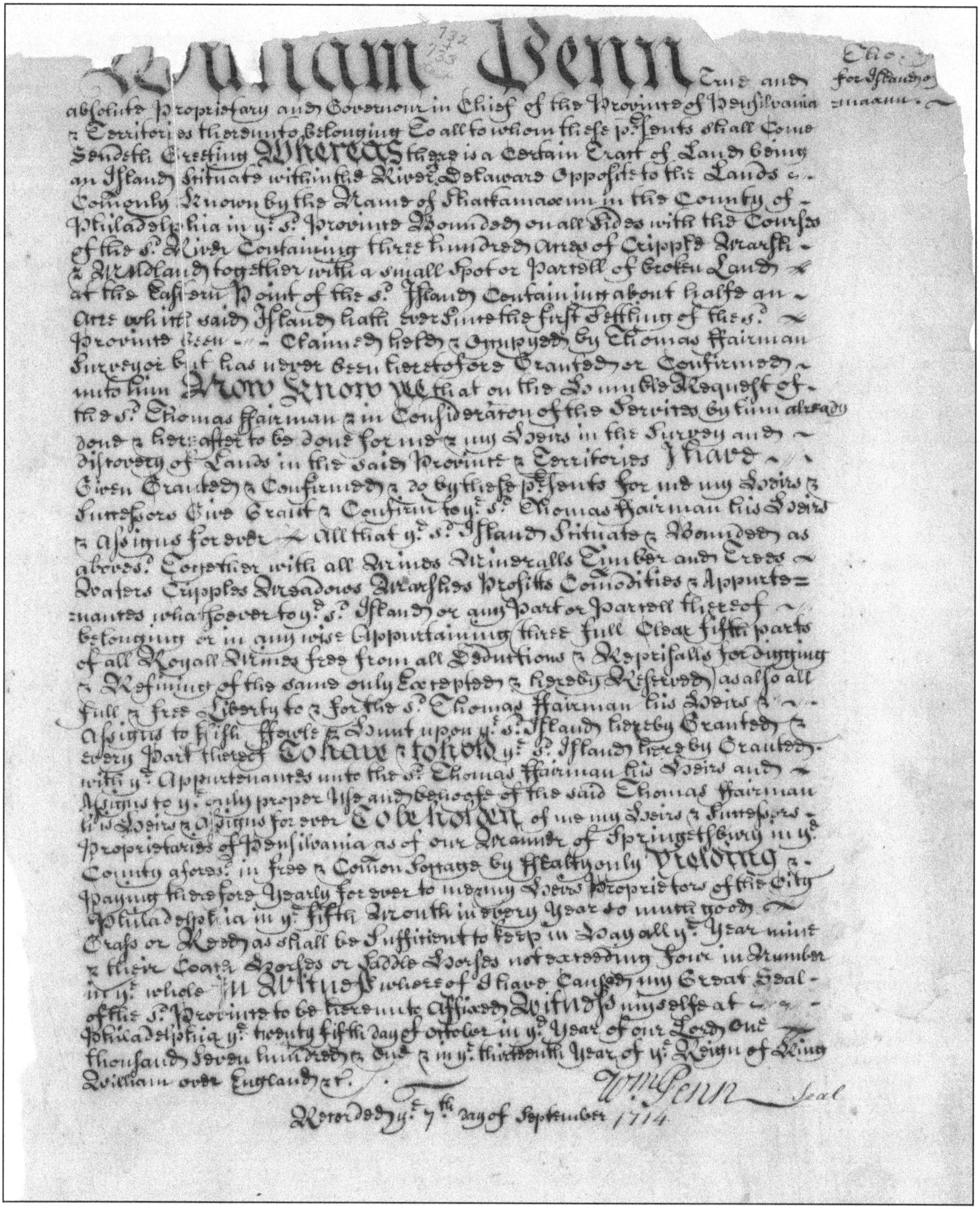

William Penn True and absolute Proprietary and Governour in Chief of the Province of Pensilvania & Territories thereunto belonging To all to whom these p[re]sents shall Come Sendeth Greeting Whereas there is a Certain Tract of Land being an Island Situate within the River Delaware Opposite to the Lands Comonly Known by the Name of Shackamaxon in the County of Philadelphia in ye sd Province Bounded on all Sides with the Course of the sd River Containing three hundred Acres of Cripple Marsh & Meadland together with a small Spot or Parcell of broken Land at the Eastern Point of the sd Island Containing about halfe an Acre which said Island hath ever since the first Setling of the sd Province been Claimed held & Occupyed by Thomas Fairman Surveyor but has never been heretofore Granted or Confirmed unto him Now Know Ye that on the Humble Request of the sd Thomas Fairman & in Consideration of the Services by him already done & hereafter to be done for me & my Heirs in the Survey and discovery of Lands in the said Province & Territories I have Given Granted & Confirmed & do by these p[re]sents for me my Heirs & Successors Give Grant & Confirm to ye sd Thomas Fairman his Heirs & Assigns for ever All that ye sd Island Situate & Bounded as aforesd Together with all Mines Mineralls Timber and Trees Waters Cripples Meadows Marshes Profitts Comodities & Appurtenances whatsoever to ye sd Island or any Part or Parcell thereof belonging or in any wise Appertaining three full Clear fifth parts of all Royall Mines free from all Deductions & Reprisalls for digging & Refining of the same only Excepted & hereby Reserved as also all full & free Liberty to & for the sd Thomas Fairman his Heirs & Assigns to Fish Fowle & Hunt upon ye sd Island hereby Granted & every Part thereof To have & to hold ye sd Island hereby Granted with ye Appurtenances unto the sd Thomas Fairman his Heirs and Assigns to ye only proper Use and behoofe of the said Thomas Fairman his Heirs & Assigns for ever To be holden of me my Heirs & Successors Proprietaries of Pensilvania as of our Mannor of Springettsbury in ye County aforesd in free & Comon Soccage by fealty only Yielding & Paying therefore Yearly for ever to me & my Heirs Proprietors of the City Philadelphia in ye fifth Month in every Year so much good Grass or Reed as shall be Sufficient to keep in Hay all ye Year nine & their Coach Horses or Saddle Horses not exceeding Four in Number in ye whole In Witness whereof I have Caused my Great Seal of the sd Province to be hereunto Affixed Witness myselfe at Philadelphia ye twenty fifth day of October in ye Year of our Lord One thousand seven hundred & one & in ye thirteenth Year of ye Reign of King William over England &c.

Wm Penn Seal

Recorded ye 7th day of September 1714

Figure 9. William Penn's 1701 patent granting Thomas Fairman ownership of Shackamaxon Island.

every yeare[.] This was a vallewable consideration and more then the Island was then worth." He said he had a particular order to Ephraim Herrman from Sir Edmund Andros and the Upland Court with a grant and warrant with Richard Noble's survey and only wanted a confirmation. He asked "how many scores of Sweads have any more for theire plantations." He reminded Penn that Andros had advised him the previous year that "m' Penn will Confirm you the Island and it is his Intrist so to doe." Finally, Fairman admitted to Penn that while he had a right to the island he also had perhaps "No firm Title in Law" and therefore requested that Penn give it to him or grant it in right of his purchase of 5000 acres from Thomas Harley.[51]

In fact, Penn gave Fairman a patent for the island in 1701, asserting that, while Fairman had occupied it since Pennsylvania's founding, Penn had never before granted or confirmed the island to him. Penn's patent granted the island, containing 300 acres, plus acres of "Cripple Marsh," at Fairman's request "in Consideration of the Services by him already done & hereafter to be done" for him and his heirs "in the Survey and discovery of Lands" in Pennsylvania. In addition, Fairman and his heirs

would provide Penn and his heirs enough grass or reeds to keep no more than four horses "in Hay" each year.[52]

While Elizabeth Kinsey Fairman held title to the island following Thomas' death in 1714 (Thomas's will stated it was originally hers and should go back to her), in 1721, Captain Charles Gookin, formerly Governor of Pennsylvania, petitioned the Board of Trade and Plantations in London to consider granting the island to New Jersey (a royal colony since 1703) and to him as, according to his description, it was "wholly unimproved and uninhabited." Cadwalader Evans filed a similar petition in 1756 also on grounds that there were few improvements on the island and that no tax was levied on the land nor any constable assigned. Both claims were denied. The successor owner to the Fairmans, Philadelphia merchant John Petty, refuted Evans's assertions with a 1741 for sale advertisement describing the 300-acre island in intensive agricultural use, including 40 acres of meadow, 30 acres cleared for corn, grain, or tobacco, an orchard of peach and apple trees, and a frame house with two brick chimneys.[53] The Delaware River boundary and island jurisdiction issues between New Jersey and Pennsylvania were not fully resolved until 1783, when six

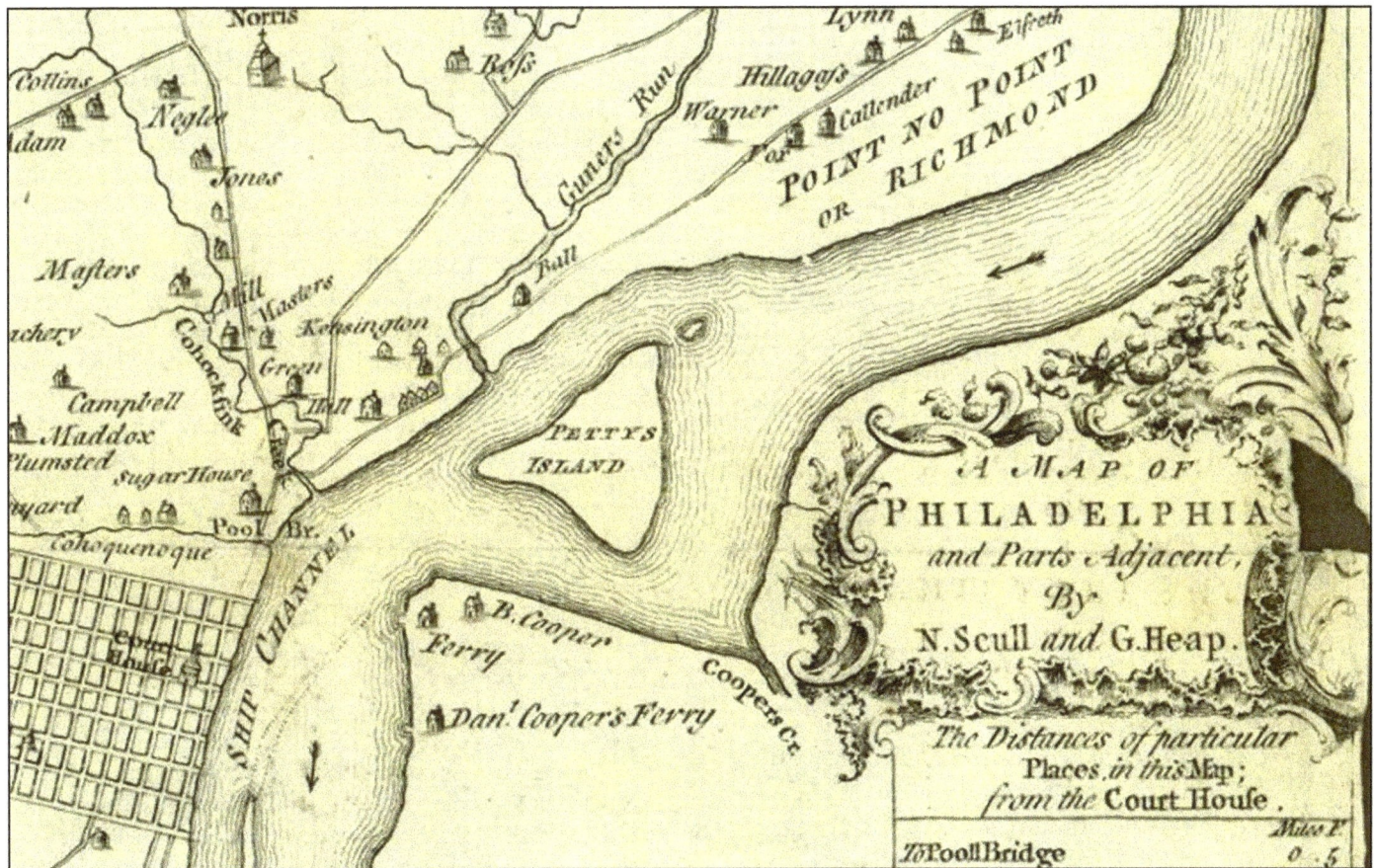

Figure 10. Detail map showing Pettys Island from *A Map of Philadelphia and Parts Adjacent* by N. Scull and G. Heap, 1750.

commissioners, three appointed by each state reached an agreement as to which islands should be assigned to each state and both state legislatures approved acts ratifying the compact.[54]

A visit today to Petty Island, now stripped of industrial buildings, offers a haunting reminder of the era before the Delaware River became a strict provincial boundary. Though much has changed after three centuries, the island's landscape evokes the Lenape towns and colonial plantations that once dominated the region. The 1678 deed for Shackamaxon Island from Wassackarous, Ojroqua, Colehickamin, and Pesacakson to Elizabeth Kinsey illuminates the region's history when Lenapes welcomed the colonists, yet expected them to provide fair compensation for land and share resources. During the early years of settlement, Europeans accepted those terms, willing to establish stable relationships with the Lenapes to gain from their knowledge of the environment and trade. Like the Indians, many colonists viewed the Delaware Valley as an integrated unit, rather than as separate provinces with opposing interests. But as the Lenape population and power declined, the numbers of Pennsylvanians exploded, and proprietors chose to guard their boundaries, Petty Island became a colonial pawn rather than shared resource.

## Acknowledgments

We would like to thank Paul W. Schopp for his ideas, careful review, and important suggestions on additional sources. We are also grateful to the many people who assisted us in research, including Bonnie Beth Elwell of the Camden County Historical Society, Sarah Horowitz of the Quaker and Special Collections at Haverford College, Barbara Price of the Gloucester County Historical Society, and Aaron McWilliams of the Pennsylvania State Archives. We also appreciate the great feedback we received from Zachary Baer, Robert Barnett, Mark Demitroff, Claude Epstein, Edward Fox, Peter Hamilton, David Larsson, Douglas McVarish, Robert Thompson, Richard Watson, John Yates, and our spouses, Roxane Shinn and Rudy Soderlund.

## About the Authors

Robert Shinn graduated Brown University with degrees in American Literature and History and Political Science. He is co-author of *Along the Cooper River: Camden to Haddonfield* (Arcadia, 2015) and three nominations for the New Jersey and National Registers of Historic Places: The Cooper River Park Historic District; the Peter J. McGuire Memorial and Gravesite; and the Newton Union Burial Ground. He is a New Jersey National Lands Trust consultant on the history of Petty's Island—leading island tours, writing scripts and producing a documentary film, and writing and narrating a self-guided island tour. He is currently writing a book on the island's history. Shinn is a member and Treasurer of the Board of Trustees of the Camden County Historical Society.

Jean R. Soderlund is a professor of history emeritus at Lehigh University whose most recent book, *Lenape Country: Delaware Valley Society before William Penn* (University of Pennsylvania Press, 2015), won the Philip S. Klein Book Prize from the Pennsylvania Historical Association. She is currently writing a book on the history of colonial West Jersey, tentatively titled "Witnesses: Religion, Death, and Memory in Colonial New Jersey," which is a social history focusing on personal and political interaction among Native Americans, African Americans, and European colonists. Her research for this article and the larger book project was assisted by a grant from the New Jersey Historical Commission, a division of the Department of State.

## Endnotes

1   Deed for Shackamaxon Island from Lenapes to Elizabeth Kinsey, July 12, 1678, Document Signed, Richard Reeve Wood papers in Quaker and Special Collections, Haverford College, Haverford, PA. In this paper, we have retained the original dates in citing documents, though the English continued to use the Julian calendar, which began the new year in March and, in the seventeenth century, dates varied by ten days from the Gregorian calendar. A further complication arises with documents written by Quakers, who refused to use the "pagan" names for months and instead used numbers, with the result that March was called "First Month," April "Second Month, and so forth. In quoting primary sources and transcribing documents, we have retained the original spelling, punctuation, and capitalization except for the thorn, which was actually not a "y" but another way to write "th." Thus, for example, we have changed "y$^e$" to the intended word "the" and "y$^t$" to the intended word "that."

2   See **1691.2** *Nova Suecia, eller the Swenska Revier in India Occidentalis*, drawn by Peter Lindstrom, Royal Swedish Engineer; 1654 & 1655. Location labeled "16" on http://www.mapsofpa.com/17thcentury/1690lindstroma.jpg. The names Shackamaxon and Treaty Island are associated with William Penn's legendary treaty with the Indians, which some historians have believed took place at the Lenape town on the Pennsylvania shoreline opposite the island's south end, in what is now the Kensington neighborhood of Philadelphia. The English used the spelling Shackamaxon and Shakamaxon, whereas Lindeström titled the Lenape settlement on his map "Kacamensi," which has been

interpreted in various ways, including "to make a chief or king place" and "the place of eels," referring to it as an important summer fishing spot. For more information about the island's transition from CITGO Petroleum Corporation to The New Jersey Natural Lands Trust, see the "Petty's Island Preserve" page on the website: https://nj.gov/dep/njnlt/pettysisland.htm.

3   Rambo's release is written on the reverse side of the 1678 deed; the confirmations are filed under Ojroqua in the Deeds file, Camden County Historical Society, Camden, New Jersey.

4   Edwin B. Bronner, "Notes and Documents: Indian Deed for Petty's Island, 1678," *Pennsylvania Magazine of History and Biography* 89 (January 1965): 111–14.

5   Herbert C. Kraft, *The Lenape-Delaware Indian Heritage: 10,000 B. C.–A. D. 2000* (n. p.: Lenape Books, 2001); Amy C. Schutt, *Peoples of the River Valleys: The Odyssey of the Delaware Indians* (Philadelphia: University of Pennsylvania Press, 2007); Daniel K. Richter, "The First Pennsylvanians," in Randall M. Miller and William Pencak, eds., *Pennsylvania: A History of the Commonwealth* (University Park: Pennsylvania State University Press and the Pennsylvania Historical and Museum Commission, 2002), 3–46; Robert S. Grumet, *The Munsee Indians: A History* (Norman: University of Oklahoma Press, 2009); Gunlög Fur, *A Nation of Women: Gender and Colonial Encounters Among the Delaware Indians* (Philadelphia: University of Pennsylvania Press, 2009); Peter O. Wacker, *Land and People: A Cultural Geography of Preindustrial New Jersey: Origins and Settlement Patterns* (New Brunswick, NJ: Rutgers University Press, 1975); Jean R. Soderlund and Claude M. Epstein, "Lenape-Colonist Land Conveyances in West New Jersey: Evolving Expectations in Space and Time," *New Jersey Studies: An Interdisciplinary Journal* 4, 2 (2018): 179–211. DOI: http://dx.doi.org/10.14713/njs.v4i2.129; Jean R. Soderlund, *Lenape Country: Delaware Valley Society Before William Penn* (Philadelphia: University of Pennsylvania Press, 2015), 12–54, 112–19.

6   Soderlund and Epstein, "Lenape-Colonist Land Conveyances," 198, 202–3; Soderlund, *Lenape Country*, 28–30; Peter Stebbins Craig, *1671 Census of the Delaware* (Philadelphia: Genealogical Society of Pennsylvania, 1999); Peter Stebbins Craig, *The 1693 Census of the Swedes on the Delaware* (Winter Park, FL: SAG Publications, 1993); Donald Einer Bjarnson, "Swedish-Finnish Settlement in New Jersey in the Seventeenth Century," *Swedish-American Historical Quarterly* 27, 4 (October 1976): 240–42; http://collections.carli.illinois.edu/cdm/ref/collection/npu_sahq/id/3710.

7   For details on the complicated transactions involving Byllynge, Fenwick, Penn, and others associated with the West New Jersey proprietorship, and the importance of the Concessions and Agreements, see John E. Pomfret, *The Province of West New Jersey 1609–1702: A History of the Origins of an American Colony* (Princeton, NJ: Princeton University Press, 1956), 65–104. Soderlund and Epstein, "Lenape-Colonist Land Conveyances," 199–202; Deed,

Meopony et al. to John Fenwick, Nov. 17, 1675, MG3 #4, New Jersey Historical Society, Newark, NJ (hereafter NJHS); Agreement of Indians with John Fenwick, Jan. 8, 1675/6, MG3 #6, NJHS; Salem Deeds #1: 42, New Jersey State Archives, Trenton, NJ (hereafter NJSA) dated March 14, 1676 "New Stile."

8   Mary Maples Dunn and Richard S. Dunn et al., eds., *The Papers of William Penn*, 5 vols. (Philadelphia: University of Pennsylvania Press, 1981–1987) (hereafter *PWP*), 1:411–16.

9   Paul W. Schopp (Jerseyman), "The Best Laid Schemes o' Mice an' Men, Gang aft Agley," published on the History—Now and Then blog at http://jerseyman-historynowandthen.blogspot.com/2010/10/best-laid-schemes-o-mice-men-gang-aft.html.

10  Samuel Smith, *The History of New-Jersey*, 2d ed. (Trenton, NJ: William S. Sharp, 1877), 98.

11  Schopp (Jerseyman), "Best Laid Schemes"; West Jersey Book B, Pt. 1: 3–4, NJSA; Pomfret, *West New Jersey*, 92–108, 124–35; Wacker, *Land and People*, 283–98; H. Clay Reed and George J. Miller, eds., *The Burlington Court Book: A Record of Quaker Jurisprudence in West New Jersey 1680–1709* (Washington, DC: American Historical Association, 1944), xxxi–xxxvii; Smith, *History of New-Jersey*, 93–95, 98–102, 124–25, 150–51; Craig, *1671 Census*, 71–72; Thomas Budd, *Good Order Established in Pennsilvania & New-Jersey in America* (1685), 28, 29, 32, 33; Schutt, *Peoples*, 42.

12  Pomfret, *West New Jersey*, 150-215, 281-82; Soderlund, *Lenape Country*, 177-83; *Historical Statistics of the United States Colonial Times to 1970 Part 2* (Washington DC: Bureau of the Census, 1975), 1168.

13  Kinsey conveyed one-third of his proprietary share to Nicholas Lucas; John Kinsey to Nicholas Lucas, April 3, 1677, West Jersey Book B: 191. He granted another third to Benjamin Scott and William Scott Jr.; John Kinsey to Benjamin Scott and William Scott Jr., April 2, 3, 1677, West Jersey Book B: 343. John Kinsey's son, John, sold the last one-third part of his father's propriety to Thomas Budd for £86 current English money; John Kinsey to Thomas Budd, December 22, 23, 1681, West Jersey Book B: 5, NJSA. The sale to Thomas Budd compares unfavorably to one-third of what Kinsey Sr. paid for a full proprietary (£116) four years before. John Kinsey Jr.'s arrival year is cited in Smith, *History of N. J.*, 103.

14  "John Kinsey Allias Kelsey Latte of Hadnam in Hartfortsheere being taken wᵗʰ a violent feavor & Payne in his Bowles about 8 days Pased out of the Body the 11th of the 8th moᵗʰ [October 11, 1677] & was Layd in the ground the 14ᵗʰ of the same 1677," quotation from Burlington Monthly Meeting Marriages, Births, and Deaths 1677–1765, 1, Quaker and Special Collections, Haverford College, Haverford, PA. Based on the description, the illness preceding his death might have been giardiasis, the most common waterborne infection of the human intestine worldwide. Edward Armstrong, ed., "Record of Upland Court; From the 14ᵗʰ of November, 1676, to

the 14th of June, 1681," *Memoirs of the Historical Society of Pennsylvania,* vol. 7 (Philadelphia: J. B. Lippincott & Co., 1860), 116–18.

15 Soderlund, *Lenape Country*; Soderlund and Epstein, "Lenape-Colonist Land Conveyances," 179–211.

16 Document Signed, Richard Reeve Wood papers in Quaker and Special Collections, Haverford College, Haverford, PA.

17 Torn. The body of the deed is written on the right side of the paper. On the left side, in the center and upside down, is the endorsement: "the indians paper for the Island ag[st] Shaksemasen." Also on the left side, at the bottom of the page, is a note: "lent Eph. Harman my portmanter" [rest of note cut off].

18 According to the *Oxford English Dictionary*, the word "mutch" in seventeenth-century English referred to a woman's cap and was borrowed from the Dutch. It appears elsewhere in other Delaware Valley documents, including a 1680 case in the New Castle court and a 1681 deed for land near Cohansey Creek. Most other West New Jersey deeds measured relatively small amounts of gunpowder in double handfuls. The Lenapes may have considered Kinsey's hands too small, so insisted on another measure. *OED*; *Records of the Court of New Castle on Delaware 1676–1681*, vol. 1 (Lancaster, PA: Wickersham Printing Co., 1904), 404; Lenapes to Henry Jenings, August 20, 1681, Salem Deeds, Book #2: 9, NJSA.

19 Overwriting results in "thise."

20 For examples of documents with accounting in guilders sewant, see Charles T. Gehring, ed., *New York Historical Manuscripts: Dutch, Vols. XX–XXI, Delaware Papers (English Period)* (Baltimore: Genealogical Publishing Co., Inc., 1977), 7–10, 51–53, 62, 65, 150–51.

21 Markham's negotiated deed with the Lenapes, dated July 15, 1682, covering the lower portion of today's Bucks County, including the site of Pennsbury Manor, was the first Lenape land sale to William Penn in Pennsylvania. Among the "summes & particulers of Goods, merchandizes, & Utensills" listed as consideration were two anchors each of rum, cider, and beer. The volume of an anchor was ten gallons. *PWP*, 2: 262; Indians to Daniel Coxe, April 30 and June 24, 1688, West Jersey Book B: 202, 203; Indians to West New Jersey Society, June 9, 1693, West Jersey Book B: 325, NJSA; Soderlund, *Lenape Country*, 137–38.

22 "From Thomas Fairman," August 7, 1700, in *PWP*, 3: 611; William M. Offutt Jr., *Of "Good Laws" and "Good Men": Law and Society in the Delaware Valley, 1680–1710* (Urbana: University of Illinois Press, 1995), 192, 213, 256; Albert Cook Myers, *William Penn: His Own Account of The Lenni Lenape or Delaware Indians 1683* (Moylan, PA: Albert Cook Myers, 1937), 85; Aaron Leaming and Jacob Spicer, *The Grants, Concessions, and Original Constitutions of the Province of New Jersey,* Second Edition (Somerville, NJ: Honeyman & Company, 1881), 512; Philadelphia Yearly Meeting (Women's) 1681–1742, 7M 1691, Friends Historical Library, Swarthmore College, Swarthmore, PA;

Jean R. Soderlund, "Quaker Women in Lenape Country: Defining Community on the West New Jersey Frontier," in Michele Lise Tarter and Catie Gill, eds., *New Critical Studies on Early Quaker Women, 1650–1800* (Oxford: Oxford University Press, 2018), 227; Budd, *Good Order Established*, 29.

23 On most Lenape land conveyances in West Jersey, a European scribe wrote the Lenape's name next to his or her mark, thus the spellings varied widely depending on the scribe's hearing and language.

24 Sir Edmund Andros was appointed governor of New York and New Jersey in 1674 and governor of the Dominion of New England in 1686 and, later, New York and New Jersey as well until 1688.

25 Grumet, *Munsee Indians,* 74, 143–44, 159–60, 169, 314, 347–48, 354; Meopony et al. to John Fenwick, November 17, 1675, MG3 #4, NJHS; Agreement of Indians with John Fenwick, January 8, 1675/6, MG3 #6, NJHS; Salem Deeds #1: 42, NJSA (dated March 14, 1676 "New Stile"); Receipt, Accomes et al. to Hipolit Lefever and John Pledger, March 27, 1675, and Deed, Meopony et al. to Lefever and Pledger, April 20, 1676, originals in the Historical Society of Pennsylvania; reproduced in Myers, *William Penn,* 60–61; West Jersey Book B, Pt. 1: 4, NJSA; Donald H. Kent, ed., *Early American Indian Documents: Treaties and Laws, 1607–1789, Volume 1: Pennsylvania and Delaware Treaties, 1629–1737,* gen. ed. Alden T. Vaughan (Washington D.C.: University Publications of America, Inc., 1979), 72; *PWP,* 2: 263; Soderlund, *Lenape Country,* 136; C. A. Weslager, *The Delaware Indians: A History* (New Brunswick, NJ: Rutgers University Press), 162–63.

26 Gehring, ed., *English,* 17–19; West Jersey Book B, Pt. 1: 3, NJSA. On the 1677 deed, the name Apperinges appears. The only known copy of this deed is a recorded abstract in the New Jersey State Archives. Of known Lenapes at the time, Ojroqua is most likely. The difference in spelling can be accounted for in Europeans' interpretation of what they heard and the copyist's interpretation of handwriting on the original deed.

27 Robert Steven Grumet, "Sunksquaws, Shamans, and Tradeswomen: Middle Atlantic Coastal Algonkian Women During the 17th and 18th Centuries," in Mona Etienne and Eleanor Leacock, eds., *Women and Colonization: Anthropological Perspectives* (New York: Praeger, 1980), 43–62; Kraft, *The Lenape-Delaware Indian Heritage,* 237–47; Anthony F. C. Wallace, "Woman, Land, and Society: Three Aspects of Aboriginal Delaware Life," *Pennsylvania Archeologist* 17 (1947): 1–35; Fur, *Nation of Women,* 1–50; Soderlund, *Lenape Country,* 78; Meopony et al. to John Fenwick, November 17, 1675, MG3 #4, NJHS; Agreement of Indians with John Fenwick, January 8, 1675/6, MG3 #6, NJHS; Salem Deeds #1: 42, NJSA (dated March 14, 1676 "New Stile").

28 Gehring, ed., *English,* 17–19; West Jersey Book B, Pt. 1: 4, NJSA; *PWP,* 2: 266; Kent, *Early American Indian Documents,* 64–67; Frank H. Stewart, *Indians of Southern New Jersey* (Woodbury, NJ: Gloucester County Historical

Society, 1932), 20, 76.

29 While Prudence Clayton's signature is difficult to read, the letters conform with seventeenth-century script. Burlington MM Marriages, Births and Deaths 1677–1765, Quaker and Special Collections, Haverford College, Haverford, PA; Craig W. Horle et al., eds., *Lawmaking and Legislators in Pennsylvania: A Biographical Dictionary*, vol. 1 (Philadelphia: University of Pennsylvania Press, 1991), 283–84.

30 Craig, *1693 Census*, 48–49.

31 Thomas's father William Fairman, a brewer in Hertford, had two other sons: Robert, who remained in England, and Francis. Like Elizabeth's father, William Fairman was persecuted for being a Quaker. He was found guilty of attending a conventicle at the house of Nicholas Lucas and sentenced in 1664 to be transported to Barbados, but instead probably was imprisoned for a short while in England. http://jeffsgenealogy.info/CookLine/g1/p1875.htm; Burlington MM Marriages, Births and Deaths 1677–1765.

32 L. Paul Dilg, "The Man Who Set Our Boundaries: The Life, Family, and Character and Work of Thomas Fairman, Quaker and Surveyor," *Old York Road Historical Society Bulletin* 37 (1977): 3–6.

33 Jeffrey M. Dorwart and Elizabeth A. Lyons, *Elizabeth Haddon Estaugh, 1680–1762: Building the Quaker Community of Haddonfield, NJ, 1701–1762* (Haddonfield, NJ: Haddonfield Historical Society, 2013); Soderlund, "Quaker Women in Lenape Country," 221–39.

34 For groundbreaking work on the vulnerability of independent women in early New England, see Carol F. Karlsen, *The Devil in the Shape of a Woman: Witchcraft in Colonial New England* (New York: Norton, 1987); and Laurel Thatcher Ulrich, *Good Wives: Image and Reality in the Lives of Women in Northern New England 1650–1750* (New York: Oxford University Press, 1980).

35 Reed and Miller, eds., *Burlington Court Book*, 1, 4.

36 Burlington Monthly Meeting men's minutes 1678–1737, 273–74, Quaker and Special Collections, Haverford College, Haverford, PA.

37 Horace Edwin Hayden and Eleanor E. Wright, "Note on the Treaty Tree and the Fairman Mansion," *Journal of the Lancaster County Historical Society* 11, 2 (1907): 64–67; Release from Thomas Fairman to William Penn, December 10, 1713, Philadelphia Deed Book D-13-474, 475, on microfilm at City of Philadelphia Archives.

38 *PWP*, 3:543; Dilg, "Man Who Set Our Boundaries," 3–15.

39 Survey 20th June 1680 – Island in Delaware since call'd Petty's Isld., Thos Fairman. 196 acres. RG-17 Records of the Land Office, COPIED SURVEYS, 1681–1912 [series #17.114] Pages of Copied Survey Book "D-79," page D-79-265 & reverse. Pennsylvania State Archives, Pennsylvania Historical and Museum Commission, at: http://www.phmc.state.pa.us/bah/dam/rg/di/r17-114CopiedSurveyBooks/Books%20D1-D90/Book%20D79/r17-114%20BookD79%20Interface.htm. It is probable that Kinsey and Fairman had decided to marry before

Fairman undertook the official island survey. They first proposed their intentions to marry at the Burlington Monthly Meeting on September 2, 1680. When they proposed a second time before the Monthly Meeting on October 6, 1680, the meeting gave them permission to marry, which they accomplished on December 24, 1680. Burlington Monthly Meeting men's minutes 1678–1737, 5; Burlington MM Marriages, Births and Deaths 1677–1765. On Quaker courtships and the process for approving marriages, see J. William Frost, *The Quaker Family in Colonial America: A Portrait of the Society of Friends* (New York: St. Martin's Press, 1973), 150–86.

40 *PWP*, 3:611; West Jersey Proprietors Papers, Minutes of the Council, Book 1:91–94, NJSA; Transcriptions of the First Quarter Century Documents of Old Gloucester County New Jersey, 1686–1710, 2 vols. (Unpublished typescript, Woodbury, NJ: Gloucester County Historical Society, 1939), 1:143–44.

41 Document Signed, Deeds file, Camden County Historical Society. On reverse: "B:E page 8. Larrance & Martha Cock. A Conveyance to Benjamin Fairman & Elizabeth Kinsey for 300 Acres of mud or Marsh on the West Side of Delaware." The document was enclosed in an envelope labeled with the name Augustus Reeve.

42 Someone inserted "90," suggesting the document dates from 1690, but the insertion is in a different hand from the rest of the confirmation and it is more likely that this document was a draft of the one below, which Ojroqua signed July 4, 1698.

43 Photostat of Document Signed, Deeds file, Camden County Historical Society. The confirmation was written on the right side of the sheet. On the left side are three notes, each written in a hand distinct from the confirmation and from each other: "Ojroqua's Confirmation of [the old?] Grant of the Island 4 July 1698." | "Pesakase is said to be the Brother of Oiraque." | "Original of this Indian deed is owned by Mr Herbert E. Reeve."

44 *PWP*, 3:612, fn 1; Document and Bronner, "Notes and Documents," 111–14.

45 West Jersey Book B, Pt. 1: 4, NJSA; Kent, *Early American Indian Documents*, 64–67; Pesacakson also witnessed two of these 1683 deeds.

46 Instructions from William Penn to William Crispin, John Bezar, and Nathaniel Allen, September 30, 1681, in *PWP* 2:120.

47 The release was written on the reverse of the 1678 deed to Elizabeth Kinsey (Document Signed, Richard Reeve Wood papers in Quaker and Special Collections, Haverford College, Haverford, PA). The release appears on the right side of the sheet and the recording information on the left: "Recorded in the Rolls Office at Philadelphia | the 9th day of the Twelfth Month 1698/9 [February 9, 1699] | in Book E 3 vol. 5 page 249 | Exᵉ ꝑ Daᵈ Lloyd."

48 *PWP*, 3:611–13.

49 West Jersey Proprietors Papers, Minutes of the Council, Book 1:101–2, NJSA; the minutes immediately following

this entry are sparse. *PWP*, 3: 606; *PWP*, 4: 26, 47–49; Andrew R. Murphy, *William Penn: A Life* (New York: Oxford University Press, 2019), 274, 281.

50 Leaming and Spicer, *Grants, Concessions*, 480–81; *PWP*, 2:390–94; *PWP*, 3:319–26; Horle et al., *Biographical Dictionary*, 1:709–16.

51 *PWP*, 3:611–13.

52 Patent A2 from William Penn to Thomas Fairman, dated 15 October 1701, in Patent Book A-No. 2, page 732 for an Island of 300 acres listed in Patent Books, Series A and AA, 1684–1781, in RG-17 Records of the Land Office PATENT INDEXES in the Pennsylvania State Archives, Pennsylvania Historical and Museum Commission, on its website: http://www.phmc.state.pa.us/bah/dam/rg/di/

r17PatentIndexes/r17-PatentIndexMainInterface.htm. Reproduction of original patent copy, Pennsylvania State Archives, Harrisburg, PA.

53 Advertisement: "TO be SOLD, an Island commonly known by the Name of Fairman's Island . . .," *American Weekly Mercury* (Philadelphia), December 10–31, 1741, 4.

54 New Jersey approved the compact by Act R.S. 41 on May 27, 1783, according to *A Digest of the Laws of New Jersey*, L.Q.C. Elmer, 824–826; *PWP*, 3:325 n. 39. Pennsylvania approved the compact by Act 1024, according to the *Laws of the Commonwealth of Pennsylvania, from the fourteenth day of October, 1700 (*Philadelphia: John Bioren, 1822), 224. The full text of "1783 Act 1024" is on the Pennsylvania General Assembly website: www.legis.state.pa.us.

**Hope Halfway**. Down in Lower Alloways Creek Township, Salem County, the waterway of its namesake widens out into a tidal marsh and meadow estuary adjacent to the Delaware River below Hancock's Bridge. The creek's sinuosity becomes much more pronounced, causing channels to be cut across the oxbows of the meanders. One of these channels is Hope Halfway, connecting the Alloway Creek with Hope Creek. Today, the island created between the meander and the channel is part of Mad Horse Creek Wildlife Management Area, but there was a time when the commercial trapping of muskrats occurred here. The bridge visible in the first postcard led from the mainland to the island, where the trappers maintained rude quarters and a half-gable shed for removing the animal's pelt. The meat was sold for use in the numerous muskrat dinners in the area, usually a fundraiser for a church. In the second image, the trappers are proudly displaying their captives. The wall of the shed is covered with pelts drying in the sun. The pelts were then sold to furriers. Trapping still continues today in Lower Alloways Creek Township, but at a much lower quantity. The township's famous photographer and postcard producer, William J. S. Bradway, captured these two images in an homage to the past.

# Captain Wilson & the Walt Whitman Bridge

Samantha Wyld and Tom Kinsella

In honor of the 200th anniversary of the birth of Walt Whitman (1819–1892), it seems appropriate to examine the history of his best-known namesake, the Walt Whitman Bridge, famous both as a regional landmark and vital connection between the people of South Jersey and Philadelphia. What readers may not know is the contribution of Captain Charles "Budd" Wilson to its naming.

Like Whitman, Budd had limited formal education. He stated that he finished the fifth grade and was often absent in the sixth and seventh grades before he was asked to leave school during the eighth grade. On a 1922 work application, he noted that he continued to study on his own. He became an accomplished autodidact, reading deeply and learning about new topics throughout his life. Over time, he became a lover of poetry, reading the greats, including Whitman, and writing poetry of his own.

In 1922, Budd became a New Jersey State Police Mounted Trooper and, in 1926, he moved on to become Sergeant of Police with the newly formed Delaware River Bridge Commission; in 1939 he was named Captain of the bridge, later renamed the Benjamin Franklin Bridge. His career there stretched over forty-two years.

It is not clear who first suggested Whitman's name for the new bridge. Captain Wilson's son was told that his father provided the name. Perhaps he proposed it to Joseph K. Costello, executive director of the Delaware River Port Authority (DRPA), although we have found no verification of that fact. What is clear is that Captain Wilson provided the lines from Whitman's poetry that were engraved on the bridge's dedicatory plaque. Bridge construction began in 1953; opening ceremonies were held on May 15, 1957; and the bridge opened to the public the following day.

The naming of the bridge was not without contention. In 1955, with the bridge under construction, Gloucester Councilman James J. Byrne complained that the city fathers of Gloucester—the eastern terminus of the bridge would be Gloucester City—had not been consulted about

Image of the Walt Whitman Bridge that adorned the invitation to "the ceremonies incident to the opening of the Walt Whitman Bridge connecting Philadelphia, Pennsylvania, and Gloucester City, New Jersey, Wednesday morning, May fifteenth nineteen hundred and fifty-seven. . . ." Unless otherwise noted, all images and memorabilia are courtesy of Captain Wilson's son, also known as Budd.

the name and asserted that Walt Whitman had nothing to do with Gloucester. He continued on. Since the Delaware River Bridge, the span that Wilson served as captain, was being renamed at the same time as the new structure, the older bridge from Philadelphia to Camden should be named the Walt Whitman, instead of the Benjamin Franklin Bridge, and a new name should be found for the span then under construction.[1]

In 1956, the Gloucester Mayor and City Council unanimously backed a proposal that the new bridge be named the Gloucester Bridge instead of the Walt Whitman. Joseph K. Costello, executive director of the DRPA, stated that "careful consideration" would be given to the suggestion.[2]

One newspaper editorial reported that the controversy had given rise to a contest that asked children "to pick a name which would redound with more honor to the state"; the editorialist offered his or her own solution: abbreviating the name to the "WW" bridge, which it was suggested could easily stand for both the (then) less objectionable "Woodrow Wilson" bridge as well as "Walt Whitman."[3] Monsignor Joseph B. McIntyre, speaking for the Diocese of Camden, suggested naming the bridge after New Brunswick native Alfred Joyce Kilmer, poet and Catholic convert, who died fighting in World War I, and was best known for his poem "Trees."

Perhaps the most vociferous opponent to the name Walt Whitman was The Rev. James Ryan, a Catholic priest whose parish in Westville, New Jersey, was about two miles south of the bridge's New Jersey terminus. Father Ryan found the name "insulting" and pronounced Whitman as "unworthy." Ryan wrote in the Camden diocesan publication, the *Star Herald*:

Commemorative medalion given to attendees at the opening ceremonies for the Walt Whitman Bridge.

> Even a cursory glance at the man and his work will reveal how unworthy he is of this posthumous honor ... As a poet he is recognized even by his more favorable critics as definitely "second rate." ... As a thinker Walt Whitman possesses the depth of a saucer and enjoys a vision which extends about as far as his eyelids. . . . A naturalist, a pantheist, a free-thinker, a man whose idea[s] were destructive of usual ethical codes—is this the name we wish to preserve for posterity?[4]

Dedicatory plaque at the western (Philadelphia) terminus of the Walt Whitman Bridge. Captain Wilson's selected lines are bottom center. Image courtesy of the Delaware River Port Authority.

# Captain Wilson & the Walt Whitman Bridge

Dr. Edward Sculley Bradley, an international expert on Whitman, disagreed with Father Ryan's assessment. Bradley was Professor of English and, in 1957, Vice-Provost at the University of Pennsylvania. During his career he would edit several editions of Whitman's poetry, serve as general editor of the 14-volume *Collected Writings of Walt Whitman* from 1961 to 1984, and as co-editor of the 1980 variorum edition of Whitman's works (an edition that untangled the complicated history of Whitman's poetry, especially his oft-reissued and reworked *Leaves of Grass*).[5]

Bradley admired the lines from Whitman that were appended to the Bridge's dedicatory plaque and, learning that Captain Wilson had suggested them, wrote a congratulatory letter to Wilson dated July 3, 1957:

> A well-informed friend has told me that you were the inspired person who selected the lines from Whitman's "Passage to India" for inscription on the Walt Whitman Bridge. You should be proud to choose so well from all that Whitman wrote. We shall now have in Philadelphia and Camden graven lines to outshine those of Emma Lazarus on the pedestal of New York's Statue of Liberty.

Here are the lines engraved at the bottom center of the dedicatory plaque:

> Lo, soul, seest thou not God's purpose from the first?
> The earth to be spann'd, connected by network,
> The races, neighbors, to marry and be given in marriage,
> The oceans to be cross'd, the distant brought near,
> The lands to be welded together.

Bradley gives preference to Whitman's verse over Emma Lazarus' famous lines from her sonnet "The New Colossus" (1883):

> Give me your tired, your poor,
> Your huddled masses yearning to breathe free,
> The wretched refuse of your teeming shore,
> Send these, the homeless, tempest-tost to me,
> I lift my lamp beside the golden door!

Wilson was touched by Bradley's letter—which he stated he would "treasure more than anyone could know"—and also by the autographed copy of Bradley's edition of *Leaves of Grass*, enclosed with the letter.

In his reply to Bradley, Wilson wrote:

> I am happy and honored, too, to have your edition of *Leaves of Grass* autographed and that will also be a cherished possession. Probably it did not occur to you, but "pocket editions" of any book are almost literally tailored to a police officer's necessities.

Captain Wilson's self-taught knowledge, love of poetry, and hard work placed him in the right position to suggest the dedicatory lines for a structure—a bridge—with out-sized impact on the South Jersey and Philadelphia communities. As we celebrate the 200th anniversary of the birth of Walt Whitman, we also honor and celebrate the man who contributed to the naming of the bridge.

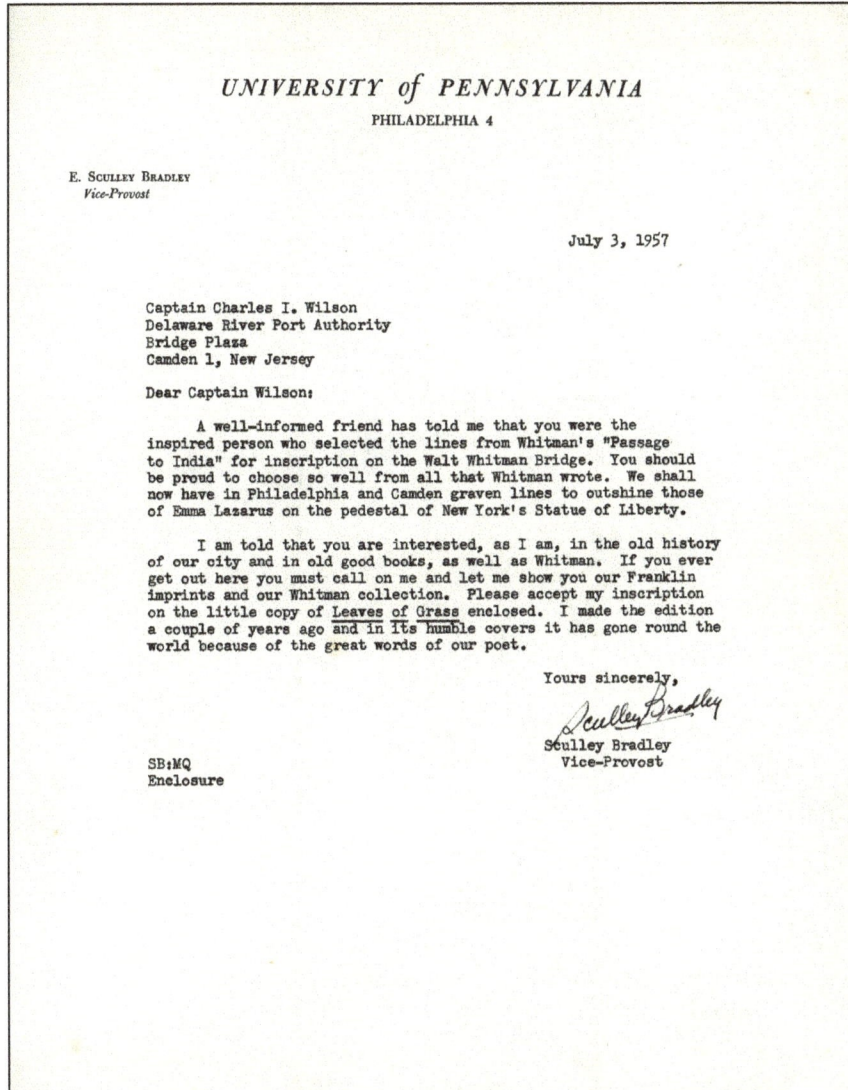

Letter from Edward Sculley Bradley to Captain Charles I. Wilson, dated July 3, 1957.

## ABOUT THE AUTHORS

Samantha Wyld is a senior Literature major at Stockton University, pursuing education certification. In Spring 2019 she was senior editing intern for the South Jersey Culture & History Center. Tom Kinsella is the director of the South Jersey Culture & History Center at Stockton University. Our thanks to Captain Wilson's son, also named Budd, whose documentation, materials, and guidance made this essay possible.

## ENDNOTES

1. "Gloucester Irked at Bridge Name," *Trenton Sunday Times-Advertiser*, August 7, 1955, 6.
2. "Gloucester Bridge Proposed as Name," *The Times-Picayune New Orleans States*, January 8, 1956, 12.
3. "The WW Bridge," *The Sacramento Bee*, February 17, 1956, 48; by way of *The Commonweal, New York Catholic Weekly*. "Kilmer's Name Urged for Bridge," *Rochester Catholic Courier Journal* (Rochester, NY), January 27, 1956, 2.
4. "Priest Hits Giving Bridge Poet's Name," *The Durham Sun*, November 24, 1955, 4.
5. E. Sculley Bradley papers, Kislak Center for Special Collections, Rare Books and Manuscripts, University of Pennsylvania, http://hdl.library.upenn.edu/1017/d/ead/upenn_rbml_MsColl1083.

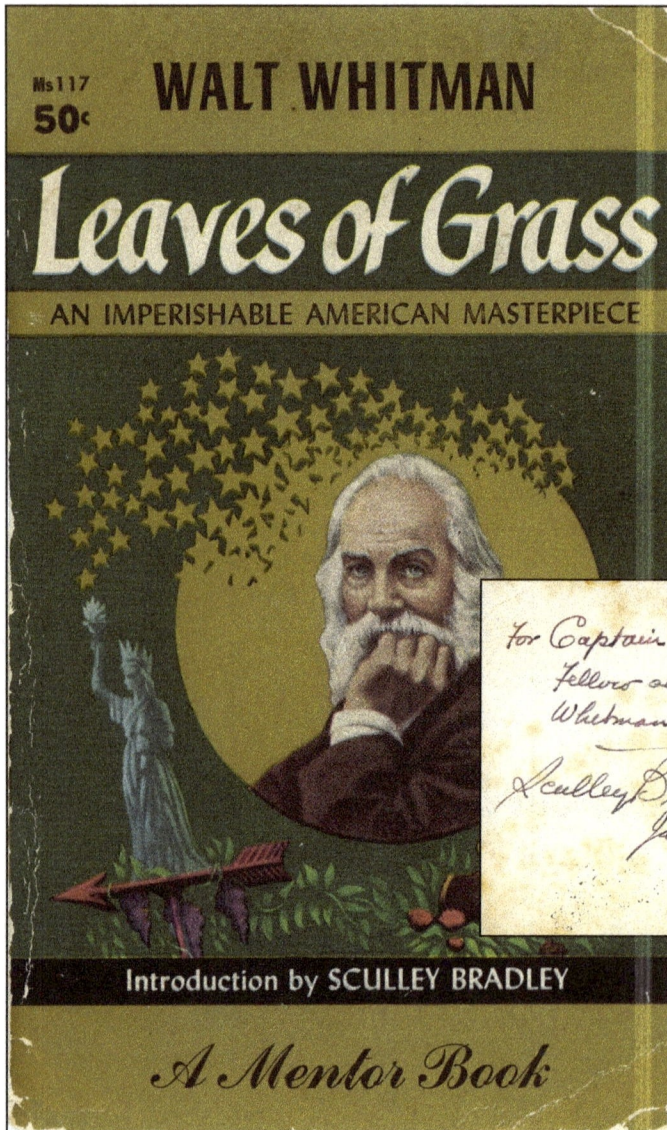

(Left) Cover of the edition of *Leaves of Grass* that E. Sculley Bradley presented to Captain Wilson. (Center) Inscription from E. Sculley Bradley to Captain Wilson. (Right) Frontispiece of Walt Whitman from a second edition of Whitman's verse owned by Captain Wilson.

Captain Charles "Budd" Wilson standing in front of the Delaware River Bridge, renamed the Benjamin Franklin Bridge at the time that the Walt Whitman Bridge was denominated. Wilson served with the Delaware River Bridge police from 1926–1968, rising to the rank of Captain.

John Simpkins of Green Bank, with his two-man saw, leans against an Atlantic White Cedar found in the Great Swamp, which stretched from the Mullica River northward across Route 542. Photograph by Arthur Hollis Koster. See John E. Pearce, *Heart of the Pines*, 722.

# Gary Giberson Talks about Cedar

### Quote: "Mullica has the best cedar"

O n April 5, 2017, Tom Kinsella and four student interns sat with Gary Giberson to discuss cedar. Several weeks earlier, Giberson had made an off-hand remark to Kinsella: "I can talk about cedar," stated Giberson, "longer than anyone would want to listen. Kinsella, a life-long cedar enthusiast, thought to himself, "Bold words." Following is the resulting interview, lightly edited.

Tom Kinsella: Well, we are sitting here with Gary Giberson in his home in Port Republic to hear a disquisition on cedar. Gary Giberson, the longtime mayor of Port Republic, has made the claim that he can speak longer on the topic of cedar than anyone would want to hear. I have challenged him on that claim so Samantha, Rachel, Rory, and I want to hear whether Gary can, in fact, tire us out on the topic of cedar. We don't believe he can.

Gary Giberson: [*Motioning toward the video camera.*] How much tape you got on that there camera?

TK: 57 hours.

GG: Okay, well I don't think we can do that. But fire away.

TK: Tell us about cedar.

GG: Atlantic White Cedar is a really a unique tree. It was the first industry of this area in South Jersey because it was so tied to shipbuilding and, of course, in the early days everything is moved by ship. It's too slow

Gary Giberson talking about cedar to members of the Stockton University Oral History internship, Spring 2017. From left to right: Rory Daly, Tom Kinsella, Gary Giberson, Rachel Baum, Samantha Zimmerman.

Edward S. Wheeler, *Scheyichbi and the Strand or Early Days Along the Delaware* (Philadelphia, Pa., 1876).

The recent formation of New Jersey, especially in the southern part of the State, is noted for extensive swamps and marshes. Those of the interior are heavily wooded, but none of them are much above tide level; the more elevated and solid are "timber swamps," and not only furnish good and desirable lumber, but might in many cases be improved by clearing and culture, and thus make valuable farms. It seems remarkable more has not been done for the agricultural development of the interior of South Jersey, but the original settlers looked to the sea for their highway, and to a great degree for their harvest too; for which reason they made their homes along the upland of the shore.

Of late, through the enterprise of several parties, notably that of Charles K. Landis, of Vineland, the interior of the State has been better appreciated, and being extensively and judiciously advertised, has attracted many intelligent and industrious settlers, who have successfully planted many fine vineyards, orchards, and farms.

The cedar swamps, which are extensive on the banks of the rivers and around their sources, are overflowed, not stable land like the timber swamps; the White Cedar (the *Cupressus Thyoides* of the botanical nomenclature), which holds exclusive possession of them, flourishes only in submerged or saturated soils. In many places in South Jersey it grows in a peaty stratum, where there is neither clay, gravel, loam or mud, but only a compact mass of fibrous roots, and the débris of its own fallen growth. In such localities, as well as where more substantial components partly form a true soil, the white cedar grows densely, and in its young growth rapidly; afterwards it becomes crowded, and grows tall, but increases more slowly in diameter.

The vegetable remains which fall from the swamp trees into the wet mass are shaded from the sun by the evergreen foliage, and thus kept cool and saved from rapid decomposition. Settling gradually down, they become submerged and then buried, from which time their decay is almost imperceptible. In this way

to move it by wagon on roads that aren't there yet, and so everything depends on shipping.

When they sailed up the Mullica River, they found this beautiful thing called an estuary. An estuary is a plot of land or a plot of water where the fresh water comes out of the lakes and streams from these cedar swamps. It starts at the roots of these cedar trees and it all comes down. Lake Absegami, Lake Oswego, and Bass River are all contributors to the Mullica River. And all of these areas produce this beautiful, fresh, clean water that looks like root beer. It has a unique color to it and it's because of the tannic acid that's in the sap that literally changes the color of this water. It has no medicinal purpose that I know of, but I've drank a lot of it because it's always nice and cold. It's usually 42 degrees coming out of the ground so in the wintertime, wherever the spring is, if you have a snowstorm, you'll see the snow all around, but this spring never freezes over. It never ices over because its 42 degrees. As it moves down the stream, the stream freezes over, but not where that spring is, and it's very dangerous when you're ice-skating on a pond that's been an old cedar swamp where there are springs. That ice is very, very thin in that area. It'll show as a white color where the spring is so you never want to skate near that.

So we're into the estuary where freshwater meets the tidewater coming in from the ocean: the bay, to the river, to the creeks, to the stream, to the ponds, and at this mixture of fresh water and saltwater, that's where you have this estuary system and that's where this unbelievable tree grows. This tree grows from the states of Maine to Florida but there's a uniqueness about this tree and you won't find this in any book that I know of because I've tried to read up on as much cedar as I can and I've come to a conclusion. I've heard boat builders and I've heard carvers and very famous people tell me there's no Atlantic Cedar like the cedar from South Jersey and I believe it's because of the climate changes from Maine to Florida.

In Maine, where this tree grows, you've got cold, cold winters and you've got trees that have a very, very narrow amount of pulp in them. If you look at the growth ring, if you slice a tree, the whole history of the tree is in those growth rings. You can tell when the winter was cold or when it was not. In Maine, the growth rings are very, very tight together and there's only a little bit of pulp between the growth rings of sap. There sap lines, that's where the life goes up into the tree.

So, what happens when you get down to Florida or you go south of South Jersey, the growth rings, because the tree can grow faster now, you have more pulp than rosin or sap—we'll call this sap but it's really like a rosin. It'll harden and crystallize. And so, when this happens the trees in South Jersey were the finest Cedar for building boats because it was right in the middle.

The growth rings on the Atlantic White Cedar in South Jersey are unique. South Jersey, because of the Appalachian Mountains, is in a climate zone that is always warmer than North Jersey—I believe that's because of the Appalachian Mountains and prevailing wind from the West.

We've got Cedar growing from Maine to Florida but the best is in South Jersey. It's so unique. I've been involved with it all my life. Port Republic is a unique example of a shipbuilding town. My family history itself goes back to 1637 and my family were Dutch shipbuilders and sawyers and when they came to the Mullica River and found this beautiful, unbelievable tree that is so good for boat building, but I'm getting ahead of myself, why this cedar is so beautiful and good for boat building.

The swamps grow extremely tight and close together. This is due to when the swamp first forms, there's all those little blue seed pods that are on the one species of sex of the tree, when they fall to the ground, they seed themselves and little cedar seedlings will come up two or three inches high. In a year they'll grow to twelve inches high but then, after that first twelve inches, the growth of this tree depends on climate; they are a slow growing tree.

There's evidence that this tree once grew to a diameter of five to eight foot in diameter. That's as much as those two tables put together. That's how big these trees were. There's evidence of these because the stumps and the hulks of them are burried beneath six foot of meadow mud up these creeks along the Mullica River. If you could go up there on a blowout tide, which you can do only with a kayak or a canoe, and get close enough to them, you can see how huge these trees were. What we had was an east coast Sequoia. Now, any tree that's that big in diameter had to be at least 180 to 200 feet tall.

You've got an unbelievable tree and you can imagine as the swamp expands, the tree drops it seedlings and all these little things are coming up. Here's the mature trees in the center. Well what happens when all these little trees start growing up, they take the sunlight away from the center trees, so the center trees grow straight and tall. There's no limb growth but I tell people cedar grows in the center of a swamp like a stalk of celery. All the limb growth is on the top one-third portion of the tree. So, you've got two thirds of the tree that's limbless, no limbs, no knots. You've got really beautiful clean boards and once shaved and sawed and lumbered, you know, and it's just beautiful for boatbuilding. They also found that this cedar when they plank boats with it and they had

the surface of the swamp is gradually elevated; a layer of more than a foot thick has thus been formed in sixty years.

The original growth of cedars were sometimes seven feet or more in diameter, and immensely high; the average size of the full-grown trees, however, was but about two feet and six inches. There are none of these great trees left, and as the whole area of Cedar Swamp is cut over every second generation, or every sixty years, a living cedar tree a hundred years old is now a rare specimen; still, the natural term of the tree is a lifetime of successive centuries. Various parties have counted the annual rings in the logs and stumps of cedars, and various witnesses affirm the existence of from five hundred to over a thousand of them in a single specimen. Sir Charles Lyell, F.R.S., quoting a newspaper article of Dr. Beesley, of Dennsiville, says (*Second Visit to United States,* vol. I page 34) that "Dr. Beesley, of Dennis Creek counted 1080 rings of annual growth, between the centre and outside of a large stump six feet in diameter;" this grew atop of a *previously fallen tree,* which was half as old; thus fifteen centuries were registered in a couple of logs on the surface of a swamp, which has been sounded in places from eight to ten or even eleven or more feet deep, and is full of *fallen* logs to the very bottom.

The white cedar, though a very tall, slim tree, sends no roots down into the firm soil underneath the swamp, but spreads them laterally in the shallow, soft, black, peaty, wet earth which is its congenial place of growth. The timber standing in a natural ancient cedar swamp is but a fraction of the quantity which has fallen and become subterranean. The living timber thus buried is apparently indestructible, and has been *mined* from its place of deposit buoyant and sound, and used for the best quality of lumber, many hundreds and perhaps thousands of years after it had grown. This mining of timber has been carried on as a regular business in the swamps about Dennisville; between nine and ten thousand dollars' worth of shingles, at fifteen dollars a thousand, have been manufactured in a year from logs thus exhumed. The production of shingles did not consume all the timber taken, as a part of it was large, fine logs, more valuable for boards, into which it was sawn. More than forty thousand dollars' worth of cedar rails and lumber are produced by these cedar swamps every year, and an acre of good swamp, fifty years in growth, is worth from five hundred to a thousand dollars. The cedars are mined not alone in the growing swamps, but in meadows where only stumps and dead roots break the surface, and in places where a smooth turf entirely hides all traces of wood from surface observation, as well in a part of the tide marshes, which were once cedar swamps, but where the growth of timber has been stopped by the encroachments of salt water in consequence of the subsidence of the swamps along the shore. Of course many of the buried trees are unfit for use. Those which grew when the swamp was shallow and the roots of the trees touched the gravel bottom, are so *gnarly* as to be unfit for splitting. Some of the trees fell only from extreme age, deadness, and partial decay: these are worthless; some were prostrated and grew long after they fell: these are hard and boxy on one side, hence undesirable. The trees wanted by the miners are those not of the bottom layer, which were *broken down* by the wind or otherwise, and buried at the perfection of their growth.

The first tool of the miner is an iron sounding-rod; with this he probes the mud of the swamp, finding often that the logs lie so thickly across one another beneath the surface that it is only after repeated efforts that he can pass his rod among them. The miner judges of the value of the log he comes in contact with after examination with his probe, by signs known to an expert only; he feels out the size, shape, and position of it, and judges of the work required to secure it; he cuts down to the log through the peat with a sharp spade, and manages to get a chip from it; by *smelling* of this chip he can tell whether he is dealing with a *windfall* or a *breakdown*, the latter being most likely to be sound lumber. Removing the peat, mud, roots, and rubbish-timber as far as necessary, the miner then saws off the log at the ends, his saw working without injury, the soil being free from grit. The log may be thirty feet long, but is generally shorter. Having sawn the log off, the miner uses levers to loosen it from its place and to throw off

the white oak here to steam bend the ribs, you know, we have plenty of white oak, even had chestnut trees here believe it or not, that chestnut tree got a blight, and all passed way. That's why it's called chestnut neck, there was beautiful chestnut trees down there. But anyway, the cedar was so beautiful and all the shipbuilding areas start in this area.

At one time in Port Republic by the 1940s, before World War Two, there were three sawmills in Port Republic. There were four sawmills in New Gretna and guess what, there was a sawmill at Stockton State College. That's why it's called the sawmill ponds and that sawmill was there to log and cut cedar, mostly for boat building. When you go into the swamp to harvest these trees and there's only one standing tree in New Jersey that I know of that's a mature tree that never got cut down and its somewhere in New Gretna and I hope your students can investigate and find that tree because its supposedly four and a half or five foot in diameter so it's a big one. And what happened to that tree because it had no growth around and it was just, I don't know, it might have been in somebody's backyard, they thought it was pretty or something that they didn't cut it down. But what happens with the limbs come out on the bottom, so it looks like a red cedar tree. Upland cedars and red cedars, that's a whole different family of cedar but it's all juniper, they're all members of the juniper family.

TK: It's the red cedar that has the beautiful smell?

GG: Yes, very unique. When I worked at Smithville, I used to take a limb, slice it and drill a hole in it and put it around a leather shoe lace and I sold them as mosquito keeper-awayers and I got a dollar apiece for them or you could rent one and bring it back and nobody ever turned them in. They kept their skeeter keeper-awayers. But red cedars are beautiful trees and as hard as a rock. It's amazing. It's a hardwood where Atlantic White cedar is a softwood.

So here we are, we're in the estuary, we got the evidence of these trees. As the swamp expands, and they will usually expand to the west because prevailing wind pushes the seed pods down a stream or away from the swamp so they'll usually, not always, but usually they'll always mature to the west.

What happens when you go in there to harvest these trees you want them great big, beautiful trees in the center of the swamp because they were fit for garvey sides. And these trees are growing six feet apart and between them, and they grow up on a hump like this, because the root system pushes the tree up, and they were very, very hard to reach and this is a period of time before Homelite came out with a chainsaw. The first chainsaw was invented or made by Homelite commercial and it weighed about 85 pounds and it was a monster, but my father chopped all these trees down—we'll get into the sawmill in the swamp later. I'll try to stay on course here because I get wandering.

So, the growth, we got the big trees in the middle, so what happened when you come in to cut the swamp wall, you started at the edge of the swamp and you cut down two little trees like this. [*Gary makes a circle with his hands about an inch in diameter.*] They make beautiful lima bean poles. You know what pole lima's are? If you are in South Jersey, you know what pole lima's are. Succotash corn and lima beans? Don't come any better with fresh butter on it, but anyway . . . getting tasty now . . . but anyway so then you got the little bean poles and then you get in and you got a three-inch log, a three-inch tree, they were cut down for fence posts, and then you get into a six or eight inch tree and this could be made into cedar shingles. There's a big, big demand for cedar shingles, asphalt is not invented yet. So, then you get into a tree this big [*about 18 inches*] and this is your weatherboard tree, cedar weatherboards. And then you finally get into this tree and there's garvey sides [*about three feet in diameter*]. Center trees would not fall—you couldn't just go into the middle and cut them because they would entangle and tie themselves up, so you had to cut the perimeter of the swamp off to get the big ones on the ground.

Cedars do not rot. They're impervious to rot. The only thing that's hard on cedar is sunlight. You take the south side of a barn, where it's got direct sunlight all year round, you'll see those shingles are weathered really hard. The grain raises, the wood pulp is worn away but the grain—the sap lines stay there so you've got sap, grain, sap, grain, sap, grain. So, you see this but on the north side, they'll sometimes moss over. They'll literally get moss on and they left the moss on them because the moss didn't hurt them, you know. It was amazing—cedar roofs would last, I would say, twenty-five to thirty years before you had to replace them and the only thing available in the past was cedar shingles. And in California they used the redwoods, you know, they had redwood shingles, but in the time I'm describing California's not even settled yet or people aren't across the high river yet, you know, so there's a tremendous amount of need to harvest Atlantic White Cedar for boat building, shingles, weatherboards, fence posts for farms. Everyone had to have fence posts.

They were also used for piling around docks. There are pilings that were put into the water and sometimes they never even took the bark off of them, but the bark will fall off the top of the piling. They put them down top first, which is really bad because the tree is tapered

superincumbent timber; this being done, the log floats upward with perfect buoyance; the under side being *most* buoyant, the log, as it floats free, always turns over. The logs for shingles are sawn into *bolts* or blocks, and *rived* and shaved into shingles on the ground. The ground is gone over again and again with success by the miners, as the logs, once disturbed, continually work toward the surface.

An inch of vegetable matter is deposited by the fall of foliage, twigs, etc., upon the surface of a cedar swamp in about five years, but as this fresh layer is itself buried, it partly decays and diminishes in bulk progressively very much by compression and other causes, so that no clue can be had from it as to the age of these remarkable swamps. Such a clue is found, however, in the buried cedars, which by annular rings tell, like a calendar, their own individual age, and by their relative positions demonstrate the successive generations of growth which must have taken place, before they could have appeared where they were left centuries since, superimposed and *grown*, one above another, in many layers.

The attempt to estimate the age chronicled by interwoven logs is confusing, but the certainty of thousands of years is evident, and even ten or twelve generations of such trees as Dr. Beesley examined may have grown and died since the oldest swamp began; and yet the age thus recorded is occupied by the most modern layer of a formation which is, in all and at the oldest, but the very latest evolvement of the most extremely short and insignificant of all the geologic periods.

If the record of ten thousand years can be preserved in mud and perishable wood, what is the chronology of the cycle in which obdurate gneiss and granite grows and disintegrates, crumbles and is recomposed of the old material, again and again, until the Azoic rocks develop into mineral wealth and fertile alluvium, tower into forests, bloom into flowers, ripen into golden harvests, nourish the beasts and birds, redden the blood of the animal world, and give strength and vigor to the body of man; the fitting tabernacle of the immortal soul? (*Pages* 111-15)

A CEDAR SWAMP, CAPE MAY CO.

The images on this page and the next are reproduced from George Hamill Cook, *Geology of the County of Cape May, State of New Jersey* (Trenton, N.J.: Office of the True American, 1857).

like this [*thicker at bottom, thinner at top*], and when the ice gets around them really tight and the tide comes up and pulls ice, that pulls the piling out of the ground so you see pilings that are raised. That's because the ice has lifted them. But when you pull a piling out, that was put down with bark on it, out of the mud, that bark will still be on that tree and underneath that bark is a smooth, shiny, white surface that nothing's ever deteriorated. Cedar is impervious to rot underwater. You can imagine what that meant for weather and for shipbuilding.

So, we've got a great demand for it. Now got cedar sawmills grow up wherever there's a swamp and, believe me, along the Mullica River, and along the Great Egg Harbor River, you've got plenty of cedar swamps. This house wouldn't be here, this farm wouldn't be here if it wasn't for that cedar tree.

As a young boy, I'd go into the swamp, we had a sawmill right down the road. This sawmill was run by a single-cylinder stationary engine. It's called a make and break engine where they only have a governor on them and the governor says how much fuel it gets and how much spark it gets and this great, big piston. The piston is this big around [*Gary shows a diameter of approximately eight inches*]. The flywheels were six foot high and to start this, you jumped on the spoke and got the thing turning, and then you went up and push the igniter on and it could be run by a little battery that big, that's the igniter—didn't even need a big car battery—and you put the igniter on and you open the gasoline a little bit and you got water going into the motor from a pitcher pump that's pumping water into an oak barrel and the oak barrel comes down with a contraption that's putting the water back to the motor and when you start the motor there's water running out of the head gasket. It's dripping water or sometimes even streaming water because that head gasket is going to expand with heat. We ain't got tolerances yet with steel or everything. It's mostly iron you know so we're talking iron against iron and so this engine fires and it's got a four-inch exhaust on it like that. Great big pipe. And of course, around a sawmill fire control is extremely important so there's rain barrels at every corner. There are makeshift little lead troughs at the edges of all the roofs and at those edges there's always a barrel there and the barrel usually has an oak stick. It looks like a great big stirring stick but it's actually oak and if there's ice on that barrel you can take that and break it loose or pull the thing up and the ice will come off the top.

So, these rain barrels always had a stick in them to take the ice in case you needed water when there was ice, because they milled all year round. If you went into a cedar swamp and cut in the summertime, which was really, really hard to do because the humidity in these swamps is unbelievable. There's hardly any sunlight that ever touches the floor so in a cedar swamp, all you have is a mound of dirt and a tree, a mound of dirt and a tree, and sphagnum moss which that's a whole 'nother thing. I'll talk about moss someday. Bring some more kids and I'll talk moss which was a South Jersey industry.

So, what happens, there's no sunlight gets on there so everything is—and it's just so hot and mucky in the summertime. You just peel your clothes off, take a great big gallon jug of water with you, you know, and as you're working in the swamp. Okay so here we are, in a swamp, and my father's got this Kelly axe. I got to use Kelly because Kelly made the best axes. They were great axes. He's got this Kelly ax, and it's a single blade ax. My father would never ever touch a double-bladed axe. Double-bladed axes were dangerous. When you set a Kelly axe down you can put it into the sphagnum moss and walk by it. If you took a double-bladed knife you set it down and you're walking and running and you're pulling with ropes and you're running around, you're going to step on that axe so that was one reason.

So, he's there chopping with the Kelly axe and the tree is like this, and you cut a V like this. First of all, you look and see which way the wind's blowing because the wind is going to help you take this tree down in the right direction you want it to fall. So you start cutting on the windward side and depending on where you start cutting that tells you where this tree it's going to fall. You start

SAWING CEDAR-LOGS, AND MAKING SHINGLES.

cutting here [*Gary illustrates a tree with his hand*] and you get halfway through and then you go around to the other side and you chop on this side and you cut in to meet it. So, the tree when its falling it looks cut like this and the stump looks like this and of course the area that's going was great big wood chips. The wood chips from that Kelly axe were six to eight inches long sometimes two inches thick. My father only weighed about 140, 150 pounds, and he had men working for him cutting, but no

RAISING, OR MINING BURIED CEDAR TIMBER.

one could chop like my father, he was amazing. He could put that tree—he could put a stick in the ground, he was so proud of working, he put his stick in the ground and fall that tree on his stick.

But one time, I'll never forget, we were cutting cedar someplace and my brother and I are watching them and there was a wind shift or something, I don't know but that tree fell forty to forty-five degrees off where he wanted it to go and it came right at my brother and I. Luckily, we had enough warning because when cut trees fall they literally scream and cry. It's an amazing thing when you chop a tree down, especially Atlantic White Cedar. This thing is like seventy feet tall and it's this big around [*approximately thirty inches*] and before it hits the ground it goes [*Gary makes a screeching noise followed by a crash*]. It just makes this great big scream that will make your hair curl. But anyway, it was always a good sound because that meant the tree was down. Now the work starts. So the tree is down in the swamp, and here comes my mother and my brother and I. She's got a plum axe. A plum axe is a beautiful little axe. They were lighter than the Kelly axe, and they had a shorter handle on them. We would start trimming the tree and we would trim all the limbs off, up to about where you could get one fence post out of the top of the tree and that would be the full of knots, so it wasn't real good. Here comes my father. On the Kelly axe handle he had a two-foot mark from the end of the axe handle, two foot, he had a notch in the axe, and he would take that and use it like an inch worm, two, four, six, eight, ten. Then he would take the axe and cut a little notch and that was the first log and then he'd go two, four, six, eight and he'd make a notch and that was the second log.

So after the tree is all limbed and Pops got her notched out, here we run with Grandpop with a two-man saw. The two-man saw it's got a great big handle on both ends. When you are cutting with a two-man saw you can't push it. If you push it, it'll bind. So once in a while Grandpa wouldn't pull to see if we were pushing. He would just let his hands off of it and if we were pushing he would really holler at us.

Here we are sawing on those trees and now you got a nice straight cut, you're not wasting too much wood. Okay now the logs are laying there, cut to length, so now we go get the truck. The truck is a 1929 Chevrolet flatbed and it had a six-cylinder engine, you know what they call the snowball engine. It had a real low transmission in it so it would just crawl and had a lot of power. Daddy—Pop he would climb up on the truck and he would reach up to us an old cedar or an oak tree, and we would put a sling around it. And he'd hook up a gate block, a gate block would go into the sling and then the

gate block would open, it would open up like that [*makes a motion with his hand*] so you could put the fall line in it and close the gate block. Now you take that end and you run it back to the woods.

Usually when they saw the tree they would use cant hooks or something like that and get the one end that you were going to attach a rope to off the ground. So all you had to do was take that three-quarter inch manila hemp rope, wrap it around, and then make a timber hitch. Even a small child like me could tie a timber hitch and I'd tie the timber hitch and I'd say, "Haul her out, Daddy!" He would put the other end into the truck, you know, and pull the logs out. That's how that they were taken out of the swamp.

When the huge logs were cut for garvey sides; we always had an order for garvey sides. We had a mill that had a very long carriage and a very long, large log bank where we could roll longer trees off and the carriage was long enough to accept these longer logs so they could be sliced into garvey sides. One piece sides for the whole side of the garvey, which was the number one work boat. When you drove a car from Tom's River to Cape May on old Route 9 about every fourth house would have garvey alongside the house. They made their living by the bay, or clamming, or whatever, you know. Fish-netting Rockfish was legal then—we won't get into that one—but anyway, we would load the truck up and those great big long logs would be put on the truck so that they would actually go by the cab and the butts would sit on the fenders of the cab of the truck, the front fenders, so you can imagine how long they were. Sometimes they were twenty-six feet long because twenty-six feet was an actual length of a lot of garveys. So we would bring them home and load the other logs in the middle and it was always so much fun to ride home on the top of a load of logs because it showed that it was hard work and harvesting and also we're sitting on a hell of a lot of money. And to have a sawmill, you know, and have the property, and to have the swamps.

My grandfather would go to these people and buy their swamps, and he would get a quit claim deed, you know, to go in there, and we would harvest the cedar off of it. He never paid a cent of taxes on it. He just let it go for taxes because he had a quit claim deed.

I remember Mrs. Anderson, she lived back in Smithville on great Creek Road, or no, Moss Mill Road, where it comes to Smithville, Mrs. Anderson. I went with Grandpa, and he's got a hundred dollar bills in one pocket, and fifty dollar bills in another pocket, in his shirt pocket. He says, "Oh Mrs. Anderson, I am so sorry to hear about your husband dying." He said, "You know he was really good." He said that, "You know, he never wanted to sell me the cedar or the swamp. I really need it, I got a lot of orders for cedar you know." And she said, "Oh no Lon, I couldn't do that! I couldn't go across what my husband wanted; he said save the swamp, never sell that swamp!" Grandpop would reach in and take out a $50 bill, and he'd fold it in half like a tent, and snap it, and put it on that metal kitchen table. And that widow woman's eyes would get real big and Grandpop would say, "Well Mrs. Anderson, you know, taxes are due aren't they?" "Oh yeah Lon, the taxes are due!" And he'd reach into his other pocket and pull out a $100 bill this time, folded it like a little tent, snap it, and lay it on down besides the $50. And after this she finally said, "Lon how many pockets you going to get into before you buy my swamp?" and he had to say, "Well my pockets are empty or that's it, you know." He always ended up getting the swamp from the widow woman.

So Grandpop would go buy the swamp and we would go cut them on weekends, because my father was a radio engineer; he built two-way radios for the New Jersey Forest Fire service in all the trucks, cars, and office headquarters and everything. They had two-way radios a little bit, a tiny bit before the New Jersey State Police had two-way radios. So my father's building all

these radios you know and he's building them on the dining room table. The house was always full of solder smoke you know, and you know how kids always want to emulate what their daddy is doing? I would take a cigar box and I would take an awl and punch holes in it, and I'd get a vacuum tube, and I'd put it in the hole. Then I would go in his junk pile where he's throwing things away and I would put that alongside with it. It would be like a transformer or something, you know, and I built little radio sets out of cigar boxes with all these junk parts.

It's amazing; I have an unbelievable memory. I have been blessed in memory, I just wrote a short story about my first day of school. From combing my hair, my brother hollerin', "The bus is coming! The bus is coming!" to coming home to my mother asking me, "What kind of day did you have?" My whole first day of school; I just wrote the whole thing. It's in my mind; I have this unbelievable memory.

But we're not talking about me or my memory, we are talkin' about cedar trees. Where are we? We're taking the cedars out and to the sawmill, and we got this great big old big stationary engine, this auto engine. My father's got the pitcher pump working,

This photograph is not the Giberson sawmill, which has fallen into disrepair, but illustrates a similar operation.

and the water is running and pouring out down on the ground around the head. Now he jumps on the thing and pulls the wheel, and she goes *k-chuff k-chuff*. You know it goes up and puts a spark on it and now, now he's got the wheels running where he don't have to jump on them anymore he can just go like this [*makes a downward pulling motion*] and pull on them because once you get a flywheel working they're a momentum-builder. So he'll pull on this, and then he goes up and puts the gas and *kapow!* this whole thing goes *kapow!* She fires and now those wheels just start spinning! Now there's a governor up on top of the thing, there are these little steel balls that go out [*makes a hand gesture showing the balls*] when the steel balls go out, that shuts off the fuel so she don't fire anymore. So when these little balls are like this [*another hand gesture*] she's going up all *kapow kapow kapow, kapow*, and these are working their way out [*another hand gesture*]. Then the balls hit the sides and she don't fire, she goes *kapow kapow kilalop kilalop kilalop kapow kilalop kilalop kapow kapow kilalop kilalop kilalop*. The noise that makes is unbelievable! It's a great big thing and to hear that sawmill start up was just, it was amazing. If we were doing something, playing around the house, and the mill was right around the pasture field there, to hear that we would always come a runnin' because we'd love to be around the sawmill. It's a dangerous thing with all the saws and everything.

The mill was set up where we could cut shingles, we could cut weatherboards, and everything, so it was a full service mill. Everything was all about cedar until World War II. When World War II ends, in the early 1950s Eisenhower is elected president and he's got this unbelievable program where he builds all those super highways and they had to have a mile straightaway where planes could land on them. This is all the I-95s and all those roads that crisscross America but also what happened was a building boom. All these vets coming home from World War II needed homes. They had married girls from France, and England, Italy, and brought their wives home or got married when they got home and had to have houses, so the housing boom was unbelievable from 1953 to 1960.

Of course then the cedar is replaced by fiberglass. Fiberglass is invented. When we saw a fiberglass boat we would get so mad, we'd say, "There goes a bleach bottle!" We called them bleach bottles because they're plastic. Bleach bottles.

Cedar had its era and it had its time. It was so rewarding to the people who lived in this area along the Mullica River, or any river, but especially the Mullica. The Mullica is one of the cleanest rivers in the country;

it's the cleanest river on the east coast! It's fifty miles long from the headwaters all the way up to Atsion, you know where Atsion Lake is? Up on 206? When you're going north up 206, which was the main north-south highway in Jersey before the Parkway, 206 goes right through Atsion. Well, Atsion Lake is the headwaters of the Mullica River. On one side of the road is the lake, and on the other side of the road is the Mullica.

And its tributaries that fed Lake Atsion—I took a canoe, I have a small, old-town canoe, it was a ten-footer. I didn't have any GPS or anything like that, I wish I would have because what I wanted to show was if you went to the headwaters of Atsion Lake from the Mullica River, how far west you could get—and Rancocas Creek coming in from the Delaware River, how close they are. Like it was a very short trip for the Indians to use the river. There's evidence that the Leni Lenape were all over and they were great fishermen. They were very close to the Indians from Virginia which were called Nanticokes. And if you go out there in this field after every rain I guarantee you can pick up a stone tool. There was something here because of its proximity to the river and everything, it's amazing, this property.

So back on Cedar, north of the Mullica, it's known as bog cedar; There's more iron deposits on the north side of the Mullica River. What happens is when that tannic acid helps all the iron form in the ground; there's veins of iron in the ground and it turns into sandstone, Jersey Sandstone. On your way out look at my fireplace, it's all Jersey sandstone. That's turning to iron, as the air gets to that stone it gets darker and darker and maybe in fifty years it will be iron because it really turns into iron. So here we got the iron cedar on that side, and then on the south side of the Mullica River we called it muck cedar because on the south side of the Mullica River the ground was richer in topsoil. I don't know why, it just is that kind of dividing line but I can literally taste a piece of cedar and taste the iron content and the amount of acid that's in it and say [*makes a tasting motion*], "this is from the north side," [*makes another tasting motion*], "that's from the south side." The professors who wrote books about the Atlantic White Cedar probably can't do that!

Anyway, I love the Atlantic White Cedar tree, it is so unique, and I take it and I meet the decoy carvers who come here to get the cedar slabs. Now when you chop a tree down it has a very large bell bottom, and when you put it in the saw, that bell bottom, the wood sometimes would be four to six inches thick. It's perfectly curved and it's sap wood and it doesn't have a lot of rosin in it. The rosin in the center of the tree holds it up but the outside of the tree is where all the life is.

## Gary Giberson Talks about Cedar

The Indians did this to clear land—guess how they cleared land? They went in and they had sharp stones and they would take and they would slice the bark all around the tree. And they'd go over to the next tree and slice all around it, they would go and do that with all these trees and five years later there was a clearing there. All those trees are dead and all over and they are great for firewood. The Indians were vagabonds, you know, they would move from one area to another; they never stayed in one place because of human waste and things like that. You can imagine what it's like to live in the woods or totally off the land. So they're moving and so it's called girdling, they are girdling the trees and taking the bark off the tree, the trees would die. So that's another way of harvesting trees. The Indians were really smart and they of course used the poles for lodges. Most of the Leni Lenape made lodges with bent over cedars and tied them with the sinews from deer. You know why deer can jump so high and so far? There's a sinew in its back leg and it's about that wide and it's about that long [*makes a thin then long figure with hands*] and it made a wonderful tying-string.

Bows were made from the cedar because it would bend really nice, or they would use oak, or birch or anything. You got an unbelievable amount of forest—the different trees that grow in the area—we have White Oak, Red Oak, Black Oak, Pin Oak, White Cedar, Red Cedar, Maples, both Swamp, Maple Gums, Sour Gums, Sweet Gums, and there are so many different kinds of trees in South Jersey it is unbelievable. It's beautiful the forest, when you walk through the forest you know, you can see the variety of trees that grow here. But nothing was as valuable as that Atlantic White Cedar. It meant so much to the economy of a growing America. They could build ships here. I have pictures of the Van Sant shipyard. They're putting four fantail, two-masted schooners together right here in Port Republic. The picture was taken off of a glass negative right around the time of the Civil War. Well I can tell you almost exactly within two years how old the picture is because my grandmother is standing there, a little ten- or twelve-year-old girl on one of these boats and she's in the dark dress, so when you get this picture that's my grandmother Laura Van Sant.

The Van Sant shipyard. Notice Gary's grandmother on the boat to the right in the dark dress. To watch the complete video of Gary's description of Cedar, visit Youtube: https://youtu.be/gdVoJcbjvV4.

Absecon Landing, Absecon, New Jersey, c. 1906. Note the cedar built garvey in the left foreground. Courtesy of the Paul W. Schopp Collection.

Van Sant shipyard in Port Republic, New Jersey, c. 1906. Courtesy of the Paul W. Schopp Collection.

Baton Rouge, La., Monday Morning, April 21, 1941.

# STRANGE AS IT SEEMS — By JOHN HIX

For further proof address the author, including a stamped envelope for reply.   Reg. U. S. Pat. Off.

### Lumber Mining.

Well over a century ago it was discovered that ancient cedar logs were buried in the muck of Southern New Jersey swamps. More important, it was found that this wood was as sound as that cut from living trees. A new industry for the reclamation of this lumber developed, and it became known as "cedar mining." The roof of Independence hall, Philadelphia, is covered with cedar shingles cut from South Jersey mined logs! Labor costs have made it less profitable than formerly.

LUMBER IS MINED...
IN NEW JERSEY!
CEDAR LOGS, 500 YEARS OLD, ARE DUG FROM SWAMPS AND USED TO MAKE BOARDS AND SHINGLES!
Cumberland County...

4-21

Above is an excerpt from a 1941 news feature "Strange as It Seems." Other hard-to-believe tidbits included a description of mutton-birds intentionally dropping to the earth; there were more than 50 time zones in the USA before the establishment of the current time zones; and in 1941 a book was returned to the Los Angeles library that was 32 years overdue—the fines, if charged, would have been $190.90. From the *Morning Advocate* (Baton Rouge, Louisiana), April 21, 1941, 11.

Stockton Seniors in Special
Collections; A painting by
R. Marilyn Schmidt.

A page from one of four vols.
of *Jersey Times* (1942–1946);
James Cooper's briefcase.

Five generations of the Lee-
Inman family c. 1923; Business
record of Evans and Wills.

## RECENT ACQUISITIONS IN SPECIAL COLLECTIONS, BJORK LIBRARY, STOCKTON UNIVERSITY

The South Jersey collections of Stockton's Special Collections have received numerous significant donations over the past year. These include additional documents pertaining to the Evans and Wills cranberry company, whose business records are held by Stockton; historic photographs of the Chatsworth area; additional materials concerning Buzby's general store in Chatsworth and Marilyn Schmidt's career; an 1830 hand-drawn map of Estell Manor (described in the Winter 2018/19 issue of *SoJourn*); a collection of issues of the *Jersey Times* and microfilm of the Atlantic City *Daily Union*; modern hand-drawn maps of Shamong, Atsion, and Brotherton; two copies of the first edition of *Migdal Zophim* (1889) describing the Jewish farming colonies of Alliance, Rosenhayn, and Carmel, along with Stockton's recent republication of this title; newsletters from Atlantic County's *Women's Coalition Press*, 1977–1983; scrapbooks from the Jewish Federation of Southern New Jersey (1940s–1960s); materials on Pleasant Mills and Lake Nescochague; and most recently a 1775 deed of land from James Pharo Sr. to James Pharo Jr.

Although Stockton's Special Collections are tied to South Jersey, not all focus on the immediate area: recently retired Congressman Frank Lobiondo has chosen Stockton as depository for his Congressional papers. Stockton has also received the briefcase used by Atlantic City lawyer James Cooper on his trip to Mississippi in 1966. Within this briefcase, Cooper kept original notes, drafts, memoranda, and photographs, as well as other contents that capture the essence of racism in the South during the height of the Civil Rights Movement. Thanks to each of the generous community members who have entrusted Stockton to preserve and make available South Jersey's local history to community members and the Stockton community alike. To see these and other collections visit the Special Collections Reading Room, E-Wing, Lower level of the Bjork Library, Stockton University.

The Reading Room is open Monday through Friday from 8am – 4pm. An appointment is preferred in order to locate and prepare materials for research. Please call or email.

Contact Heather Perez
Special Collections Librarian & University Archivist
609-652-4532 (Reading Room)
609-652-4555 (Office)
Heather.Perez@stockton.edu

# Railroads and Forest Fires

Horace A. Somes Jr. and Paul W. Schopp

Since the dawn of the railroad age and through to the end of steam propulsion, the release of sparks and embers from the locomotive and train was a constant and dangerous hazard, causing untold conflagrations. Prior to the use of coal as fuel, railroads in the United States employed cordwood to provide the necessary heat for creating steam in the boiler. The use of wood proved the most hazardous of all, since the smokestacks would often disgorge chunks of flaming wood, setting grasslands, woodlands, and buildings ablaze on a regular basis. Mechanical engineers and locomotive builders sought ways to limit the discharge of combustion sources through lengthening the boiler's smokebox in an effort to catch larger pieces of wood, and creating smokestacks with screening and a variety of elaborate ember and spark traps within the metal sheeting of the stack. In an 1860 patent infringement trial involving Matthias Baldwin, Philadelphia's most famous locomotive builder, he had his draftsmen prepare a diagram of the major spark arresting smokestack patents awarded through 1859 (Figure 1). Many of these stacks designs, derived from the fanciful ideas of inexperienced tinkerers, proved useless in practical application.[1]

Not only did the locomotives take a heavy toll

on the waysides adjacent to the railroad, but the passengers themselves endured damage to their clothing and burns to their skin with the coach windows wide open in the summer and witnessed the effect of embers with the windows closed in the winter. An angry passenger once penned a letter to an unnamed railroad company, asking,

> Is there a single person, who has traveled on any other road in the United States, on which locomotives are used, with wood for fuel, that has not been annoyed, and either had his flesh or clothing burnt? . . . Baggage cars have burnt, passenger cars have been on fire, and ladies almost denuded.[2]

Charles Dickens, writing in his work *American Notes*, first published in 1842, described the maelstrom he glimpsed through a coach window of a Boston & Lowell train in the winter as "a whirlwind of bright sparks, which showered about us like a storm of fiery snow."[3] Paul Schopp, one of the authors of this article, recalls a story his father told about Great Uncle Joe Detterer, who rode to Atlantic City in the summertime on the narrow-gauge Philadelphia & Atlantic City

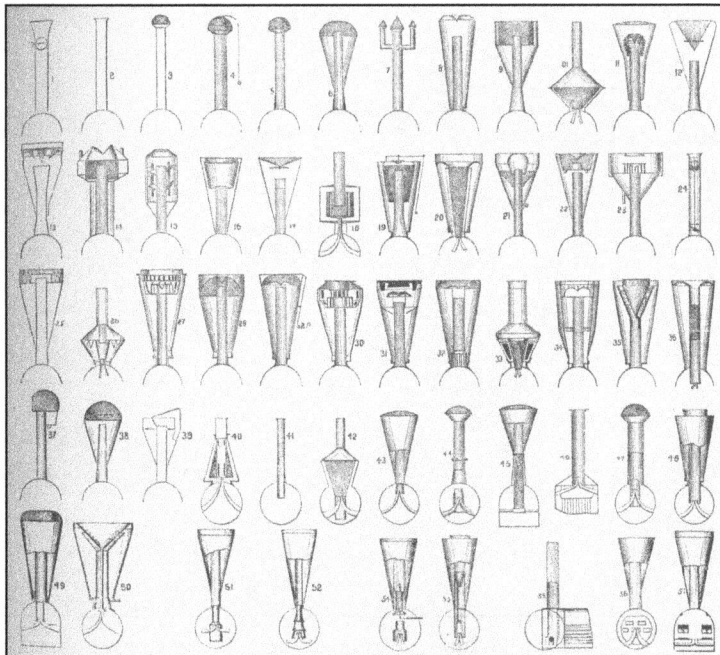

Figure 1: Reproduced in White, 1968, 115.[1]

Railway. Riding with the all the coach windows open for ventilation behind a wood-burning locomotive, Mr. Detterer recounted that he arrived at the seaside resort with large holes burned in clothing and by the time he arrived back in Philadelphia, he barely had any clothes left hanging on his body!

As wood yielded to the more efficient and abundant coal as a fuel for the locomotive, smokestack and smokebox designs became simplified and large chunks of burning wood no longer escaped to create mayhem. The overall risk of fire remained high, however, even from coal-burning locomotives. Burning embers still escaped the smokestack and hot coals often dropped between the rails from the grates and ashpans under the firebox. Sparks emanating from braking also ignited many fires, as did overheated wheel bearings.

The railroads in New Jersey that extended to the coast and elsewhere through the Pine Barrens beginning in the mid 1800s brought regional transportation to the area. Wood and coal burning engines and cars with brakes and bearings that could overheat, however, produced embers that would ignite forest fires in the flammable pines. This brought a new cause of wildfires to the forested region already subjected to wildfires that could extend across the "barrens" through the interior towns to the coastal communities.

The frequent fires occurring in New Jersey caused by the state's various railroads sparked the New Jersey State Legislature to action. In April 1865, the lawmakers passed legislation titled "An act to prevent injuries by fire from locomotive engines on railroads, and to provide for compensation therefor." The first paragraph in the act includes the following verbiage:

> That it shall be the duty of every railroad company in this state, and of every company or person operating or using any railroad in this state, with a locomotive engine or locomotive engines, to take and use all practicable means to prevent the commu-

nication of fire from any locomotive engine used or employed by them or any railroad in this state, in passing along or being upon any such railroad to any property of whatever description or any owner or occupant of any land adjacent or near to such railroad.[4]

The act also names the railroads as libel for damages from any fire proven to emanate from a locomotive or train. Subsequent legislatures passed supplements to this 1865 act, but despite the lawmakers' best intention to decrease the number of fires through the passage of this act, the conflagrations wrought by locomotives and trains never really diminished.

The April 16, 1874, edition of the *Monmouth Democrat* provides a summary of the New Jersey State Board

Figure 2: Although prepared to show the New Jersey Central's Southern Division and its branches (shown in red), this map also depicts the other rail lines that crisscrossed through the forests of southern New Jersey.

Figure 3. Our artist's sketches of the recent forest fires in New Jersey: 1) The flames in a swamp. 2) Going through fire. 3) Rescuing the animals. 4) Scene at night. The artist was Frank H. Taylor; from the *Daily Graphic* (New York), September 9, 1874, 4.

of Agriculture's first annual report, including the following narrative on forest fires within southern New Jersey:

> The losses by forest fires are very heavy and discouraging to all owners of pine lands and other large tracts in wood. Dr. Price, of Tuckerton, says that one million acres has been burned over within a few years. A single fire has been known to sweep over thirty thousand acres. Dr. Wales, of Tuckahoe, considers the reduction in the *saleability* [sic] of such exposed woodland amounts to two hundred per cent., and Dr. Price says, that "pine lands once considered valuable for the growth of timber, have become to be regarded about as insecure as any property a man can own." Formerly these fires started from coalings, or from burning brush, sedge, grass, &c. &c., but latterly the most frequent source is in sparks from locomotives. Not only do these fires, so frequently occurring, burn the timber; they also rob the soil by consuming the leaf mould and these wide parched and burnt areas invite droughts, making the country "a blackened desert." Legislation seems necessary to prevent the ravages of so frequent fires, or at least to restrict them within narrow limits in case they get started.[5]

Camden's *The Morning Post* dedicated a half column on the first page of its April 15, 1880, edition to the forest fires then sweeping Cumberland, Atlantic,

and Ocean counties. Near New Egypt, the fire left a path of pure destruction measuring 50 miles in length and 10 miles wide. As noted in the first article, "The fire originated from a spark from a locomotive on the New Jersey Southern Railroad yesterday morning." In another piece from Toms River in the same column, the stringer reports, "The fire is said to have originated from the wood burning locomotives on the Tuckerton Railroad."[6]

The frequent forest fire articles appearing in the state's various newspapers provide a strong witness to the continuum of economic and personal loss to New Jersey's property owners, causing state agencies, primarily the New Jersey State Geologist, to take an increasingly active role in prevention through scientific forest management techniques and proactive firefighting. The State Geologist's 1898 annual report contains a 100-page appendix titled "A Study of Forest Fires and Wood Production of Southern New Jersey."[7] Forester Gifford Pinchot prepared this appendix and most authorities view Pinchot as the father of scientific forest management. The appendix includes recommendations for an organized response when and where fires occur. It also provides an example for the simulated detection, communications, and suppression of a wildfire at Speedwell, Burlington County. This effort relied upon personnel and facilities positioned geographically at railway locations in Egg Harbor City, Atlantic County, and at Tuckerton, Ocean County. The rail system provided not only a means of transportation for firefighters, but also communications via the lineside telegraphs. The following year, the New

# THE PENNSYLVANIA RAILROAD COMPANY

PHILADELPHIA, BALTIMORE & WASHINGTON RAILROAD COMPANY
NORTHERN CENTRAL RAILWAY COMPANY
WEST JERSEY & SEASHORE RAILROAD COMPANY

## THE PREVENTION AND EXTINGUISHMENT OF FOREST AND GRASS FIRES

In order to prevent as far as possible the occurrence of Forest and Grass Fires and eliminate the damage which they cause, stringent measures for their prevention and suppression must be taken during the season of fire danger before vegetation starts in the spring and after it dies in the fall, and during periods of dry weather at any time. Beginning about March 1st and October 1st of each year, special vigilance must be exercised until the season of fire danger is passed, and Supervisors, track foremen, and others must be governed by the following regulations:

1. Trackmen shall burn old ties and other debris at such time and in such places as will not result in any spread of the fire.

2. Enginemen shall use every precaution against fire and not permit burning waste, hot cinders, or any other inflammable material to be thrown or dropped from the engine; clean the ash pan or front end only at points specially designated; and report promptly any defects in the devices on locomotives designed to prevent the throwing of sparks or dropping of hot coals.

3. Trainmen shall place fusees only where there is no likelihood of fire spreading from them.

4. Trackmen shall promptly extinguish all fires which start on or near the right-of-way, and render all possible assistance in fighting fires whether on private land or on property owned by the Company.

5. Trainmen shall notify the first section gang passed and report to the Superintendent from the nearest telephone or telegraph, the existence of fires which evidently have not previously been discovered or had no steps taken toward their extinguishment. Freight trainmen shall, wherever practicable, stop and extinguish small fires, since waiting to report them might give them time to get beyond control. Other employes will take the necessary steps to notify the Superintendent and trackmen of such fires as come to their notice.

6. Supervisors shall have all grass, brush, and debris within the right-of-way line opposite the forest plantations, and, when feasible, as far back as the plowed fire line (which will be 100 feet from the track wherever possible), burned in the fall of each year as soon as the grass has died down enough to make this possible. Wherever practicable, the same plan of burning shall be followed on the right-of-way where there are no forest plantations. This burning shall be done with extreme care, and only when there is a calm or when the wind is blowing toward the track; and sufficient men shall be kept on the work to prevent the fire spreading to adjoining property.

7. If a large fire occurs on land not owned by the Company, the Supervisor shall notify the nearest State Fire Warden. In case he cannot be located and the fire is in Pennsylvania, notify the Commissioner of Forestry at Harrisburg; if it is in Maryland, notify the State Forester at Baltimore; if it is in New Jersey, notify the State Forester at Trenton. The names and addresses of the Fire Wardens for the various districts will be furnished prior to each season of fire danger.

8. Operators shall transmit without charge, as Company business over Company lines, all messages relating to forest, woodland, or grass fires which are on or near Company property or are likely to affect Company property.

### GENERAL INSTRUCTIONS

Remember that the most effective means of controlling forest fires is to prevent them. Use great care in the use of fire in forests or grass lands. Do not throw burning matches or tobacco where they can set fire, and impress others with the necessity for following these precautions.

If a fire starts, take prompt and energetic action to prevent its getting beyond control, and make use of the telephone, telegraph, or other means of getting help when it is needed. Plan definitely what action to take and how much help will be needed; a few men properly directed will accomplish much more in extinguishing a fire than a large force working at random.

After a fire is controlled, guard it until it is entirely extinguished. Not even a spark should be left where fire might start. Fires which have been thought to be under control have broken out afresh with a change in the wind. It is safe to watch a woods fire twenty-four hours after it is seemingly out.

Fight light grass fires and ground fires in the woods with green boughs, brooms, wet burlap, or by throwing on fresh dirt. If the line of flame is too hot for this, try scraping or digging a trench around the fire. Take advantage of natural vantage points, such as rock outcrops, streams, roads, etc., and connect them with lines or trenches along which the mineral soil is exposed. In severe fires start back-firing toward the approaching main fire from a break or line of some kind. For the ordinary ground fire the tools most readily available—the axe, hoe, shovel, water bucket, and burlap bag—are usually sufficient.

The fundamental object in suppressing forest fires is to protect property, particularly buildings, fences, timber, forest plantations, etc. It should also be remembered that the suppression of fires is an essential step in the conservation of our forest and water resources. The various States have fire laws and organizations to fight them. The States alone, however, cannot at present suppress all fires, and it is obviously the duty of all land-owning individuals and corporations to help create a public sentiment adverse to fires and to take all possible action in their power to curb the fire evil.

FEBRUARY 1, 1912                                        SUPERINTENDENT.

Badly burned Pine, with stunted Oak sprouts underneath. From the *Annual Report of the State Geologist for the Year 1898* (Trenton, 1899), Appendix, after page 36.

Repeatedly burned land, with sprouts of Oak and Pine, Tuckerton, New Jersey. From the *Annual Report of the State Geologist for the Year 1898* (Trenton, 1899), Appendix, after page 36.

Jersey State Geologist published a two-volume annual report with the second volume being totally dedicated to the care and preservation of the state's forests. The forest report featured a number of authors, and repeats relevant portions of Pinchot's text featured as an appendix in the 1898 report.[8]

The 1902 Annual Report of the State Geologist included a description of a 75,000-acre wildfire that a Central Railroad of New Jersey locomotive ignited in May 1902 at Woodmansie, Burlington County. The fire spread with the prevailing westerly wind for a distance of twenty miles southeasterly towards the coast to Little Egg Harbor. After burning for three days, rainfall finally extinguished the fire, but it destroyed some fine stands of pine and cedar timber. No human intervention occurred with this conflagration other than to protect habitations and businesses.[9]

A state law passed in March 1905 established the Forest Park Reservation Commission within New Jersey government. The legislature sought to institute scientific forest management in New Jersey and also likely deemed it appropriate to relieve the state geological survey of most responsibilities concerning forest fires, although the state geologist was a permanent member of the commission's governing body.[10] The first annual report recaps the forest fires in the state for the years 1902, 1903, and 1904.

| Locomotive Ignited Forest Fires in South Jersey for 1902, 1903, and 1904[11] | | | | | | | | |
|---|---|---|---|---|---|---|---|---|
| | Atlantic | Burlington | Camden | Cape May | Cumberland | Gloucester | Ocean | Salem |
| 1902 | 7 | 2 | 1 | 9 | 1 | 0 | 1 | 0 |
| 1903 | 6 | 2 | 0 | 2 | 1 | 1 | 3 | 1 |
| 1904 | 3 | 4 | 4 | 5 | 0 | 0 | 1 | 3 |

In the forest commission's second annual report, William Chew, secretary for the body, reported the following:

> It can be said that the most important work accomplished by the Commission during the year has been the inauguration of the Forest Fire Service. The Commission prepared a bill providing for the appointment of fire wardens and the prevention of forest fires, and presented it to the Legislature. . . . It passed the Legislature and became a law by the approval of the Governor,

April 18, 1906. The law did not go into effect, however, until July 4 last, at which time the Commission appointed Theophilus P. Price, of Ocean county, State Fire Warden, and began at once the organization of the fire service throughout the wooded parts of the State.[12]

The 1906 enabling legislation for the state fire warden authorized him to request the appointment of local and district fire wardens in the 81 fire zone municipalities. The annual report for that same year provides a list of the first such fire wardens. In March 1907, the state legislature passed a supplement to the fire warden law, allowing the state level fire warden to ask New Jersey's various railroads to appoint section gang foremen as additional fire wardens, bringing the total number of forest fire officers to 272 in defined fire districts across the state.[13]

The railroad section foremen, when doubling as fire wardens, not only reported and responded to fires along the railway, but also clear cut adjacent to the tracks to keep the right-of-way clear of hazardous brush and trees that could be ignited by embers or sparks from passing trains. The 1907 annual report notes,

> The number of fires set by locomotives in this State is very great, although it is probable that not all the fires attributed to the railroads are actually set by them. A reason for this is easily found in the fact that many trains scheduled to run at high speed traverse the pine section where a spark easily finds something to burn. Since the number of fires due to brush-burning has been reduced the proportion started from locomotives

### The WOODMANSIE-OCEAN COUNTY WILDFIRE of 1902

"May 9th, 1902. Locomotive sparks started a fire near Woodmansie, which burned 75,000 acres, one-third in Burlington, two-thirds in Ocean County. This fire spread in a southeasterly direction to the coast, lasting three days on one wing, and ten days on the other, and burning over twenty miles long and from one to eight miles wide. The little village of Jungs Neck was in great danger of being destroyed. The fire was finally extinguished by rain, after burning some fine pine and cedar timber. No effort was made to extinguish the fire except where it threatened the village of Jungs Neck. Average loss, $1 per acre; total, $75,000."

From the *Geological Survey of New Jersey, Annual Report of the State Geologist for the Year 1902*, Part III. "Forest Fires in New Jersey During 1902" (abstract from Burlington County, p. 101).

# Railroads and Forest Fires

has increased greatly. . . . [T]he railroads themselves are seeking to remedy the evil on account of the many claims for damages that are brought against them. That many of these claims are unjust is but another reason for removing the cause upon which they are based. It is thus a fact that some of the roads, notably the Pennsylvania, are clearing their rights-of-way and adopting other measures to prevent fire being set from their locomotives.

But it is not enough to leave this great evil to be remedied by the voluntary action of the railroads.

The State should require the construction and maintenance of protective strips along every railroad that traverses woodland, on the same ground that it requires the farmers to get permits for burning brush on their own land—the general welfare.

The width and manner of making these fire breaks will vary in different parts of the State; the important feature is to secure a strip of bared earth not less than six feet wide beyond the range of falling sparks. The remainder of the fire break should be kept reasonably free of combustible

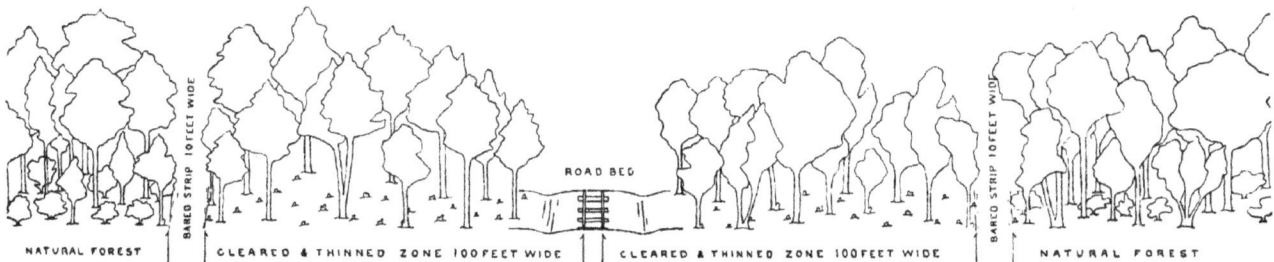

FIG. 4.—DIAGRAM OF RAILROAD FIRE LINE CONSTRUCTED ON LEVEL GROUND ACCORDING TO CHAPTER 74, LAWS OF 1909.

(Top) Diagram of railroad fire line constructed on level ground according to chapter 74, Laws of 1909. (Bottom) Railroad with fire lines on each side, Pennsylvania Railroad, east of Browns Mills Junction, February 8, 1910.

matter by frequent removals of the grass and brush, but scattered trees need not be disturbed. I doubt if the roads themselves will oppose such a measure, if it is framed carefully and with reasonable consideration for all interests. Certainly the question demands immediate consideration, for the railroads are now the greatest menace to our woodlands.[14]

Using the Tuckerton Railroad as one example of the need to reduce forest fires from locomotives and trains, the annual report of the forest commission for 1907 listed the following fire wardens for the Tuckerton Railroad:

Frank Gale – Tuckerton
William H. Blake – Barnegat
Charles Earley – Whiting[15]

Two years later, the annual forest report indicates that the lineside clear cut safety buffer for the Tuckerton Railroad needed to be established for seven miles, mainly along the eastern side between Bamber and Tuckerton.[16] The 1910 annual report contained photographs of not only firefighting equipment and a railway car, but an early lookout that could be used by fire wardens as well as postal mail carriers on their rural routes.[17] The 1914 annual report indicates that the Tuckerton Railroad had 38 miles of forest exposure. The annual responsibility for forest fires states that five ignitions were chargeable under the Forest Fire Law—with claims made and paid for three of the fires by the Tuckerton Company.[18]

Discussion of the history of railroad-related forest fires in South Jersey could easily fill an entire issue of *SoJourn*. In an effort to bring closure to this brief sketch, let us move forward in time to May 14, 1977, when a train on the Central Railroad of New Jersey caused numerous fires from High Crossing, at the old Tuckerton-Hampton Gate Road, to Woodmansie, near Route 72. Although the locomotive operated on diesel fuel, a mechanical problem in a wheel bearing or the braking system emitted sparks that ignited lineside fires. Creation of new fires ended when the New Jersey Forest Fire Service halted the train, and effectively controlled the array of lineside fires—although a major fire of 720 acres did burn east of Chatsworth.[19] In an earlier era, this could have resulted in a conflagration similar to Woodmansie in 1902, described above, before the state had an organized approach to addressing fires.

Today the Tuckerton and Jersey Central railroads are long gone; however, forest fires remain a threat to both coastal and inland communities—particularly as new people build in forested areas. Among the many commu-

nities in and around the Pine Barrens, both Tuckerton and Little Egg Harbor remain exposed to wildfire hazards. In 1930 and again in 1970, fires burning through the Wharton Tract threatened to spread with prevailing winds to the east and the coast. The 120,000-acre conflagration in 1930, bounded between the Batsto and Bass rivers, was prevented from expanding due to a smaller 20,000-acre fire that had occurred the previous week and burned from New Gretna, Burlington County northward to Munion Field—west of County Route 539.[20]

## ABOUT THE AUTHORS

Horace A. Somes Jr. is a resident of Turtle Creek Neck, Wading River, Washington Twp., Burlington County, at a homestead farm owned by the McAnney family for the past century, with six generations dating back in the region to the 1800s at Batsto. He retired from the New Jersey Forest Fire Service as Division Firewarden for the central region of the State from the Raritan to Mullica Rivers, and previously served as Section Firewarden responsible for wildfire suppression, investigation and prevention in the Wharton Tract/Penn Forest core of the Pine Barrens. He continues public services to the local community through membership in volunteer fire-rescue and emergency medical companies. He is also co-owner with his brother Frank of a family business that continues to farm the property for Christmas trees. He has had a lifelong interest in natural and human history, the Jersey Coast and Pinelands, and made contributions to John E. Pearce's *Heart of the Pines*.

New Jersey railroad history has always held a special attraction to Paul W. Schopp, probably due in part to his father's employment with the Pennsylvania Railroad. A co-author of *The Trail of the Blue Comet*, Paul understands how the railroads transecting the Pine Barrens presented a special danger to maintaining a healthy status quo among the trees of the area. Paul is the Assistant Director of the South Jersey Culture & History Center.

## ENDNOTES

1 John H. White Jr., *American Locomotives: An Engineering History, 1830–1880* (Baltimore: Johns Hopkins Press, 1968), 114–22.

2 Ibid., 114.

3 Charles Dickens, *American Notes for General Circulation*, Volume I, Second Edition (London: Chapman and Hall, 1842), 165.

4 *Acts of the Eighty-Ninth Legislature of the State of New Jersey* ... (Newark, NJ: Newark Printing and Publishing Company, 1865), 901.

5 "First Annual Report of the State Board of Agriculture; Forest Fires," *Monmouth Democrat* (Freehold, NJ), April 16,

1874, 1.

6 "Forest Fires," *The Morning Post* (Camden, NJ), April 15, 1880, 1.

7 *Annual Report of the State Geologist for the Year 1898* (Trenton, NJ: MacCrellish & Quigley, 1899), Appendix 1-100.

8 *Annual Report of the State Geologist for the Year 1899: Report on Forests* (Trenton, NJ: MacCrellish & Quigley, 1900), 103–35.

9 *Annual Report of the State Geologist for the Year 1902* (Trenton, NJ: The John L. Murphy Company, 1903), 101.

10 *First Annual Report of the Forest Park Reservation Commission of New Jersey* (Trenton, NJ: MacCrellish & Quigley, 1906), 9–12.

11 Ibid., 25–27.

12 *Second Annual Report of the Forest Park Reservation Commission of New Jersey* (Trenton, NJ: MacCrellish & Quigley, 1907), 13-14.

13 *Third Annual Report of the Forest Park Reservation*

*Commission of New Jersey* (Trenton, NJ: MacCrellish & Quigley, 1908), 50–52.

14 *Second Annual Report*, 57–58.

15 Ibid., 82.

16 *Fifth Annual Report of the Forest Park Reservation Commission of New Jersey* (Trenton, NJ: State Gazette Publishing Company, 1910), 38.

17 *Sixth Annual Report of the Forest Park Reservation Commission of New Jersey* (Paterson, NJ: News Printing Company, 1911), 50.

18 *Tenth Annual Report of the Forest Park Reservation Commission of New Jersey* (Camden, NJ: S. Chew & Sons Company, 1915, 55).

19 "Berkeley Fire Cause Probed; 800 Moved Out," *Asbury Park Press* (Asbury Park, NJ), May 16, 1977, 1.

20 "Forest Fire Peril Now Confined to Woods at Batsto," *Evening Courier* (Camden, NJ), May 6, 1930, 25.

## IDENTIFYING THE CORRECT GREENWICH TEA HOUSE

Visiting the Cumberland County Historical Society last fall, I asked Warren Adams what he thought about the Summer 2018 issue of *SoJourn*. He made a few polite observations. When I pressed him, asking whether he had seen the short piece on the Greenwich tea house (*SoJourn* 3.1, p. 30), he replied "Yes, but you identified the wrong house."

In that summer issue, the editors of *SoJourn* had reproduced an early twentieth-century postcard which identified an unnamed, obviously older home as the "Tea House, Greenwich, N. J." In his brief piece "Retiring the Tea House Myth," published in the *Cumberland Patriot*, Spring 2019, Adams writes: "For over one hundred years, the house at 1036 Ye Greate Street, now Down Jersey Marine Services, has been called the 'Tea House.' The picture that has graced many a postcard and spots in much printed material has finally been retired." Adams describes a letter in the collection of Sara Sheppard Hancock, longtime President of the CCHS, that provides more definitive details. The letter writer, Charles Ewing, describes details of the tea burning raid that his grandfather, Wm. B. Ewing, heard from his father, Thomas Ewing, one of the Patriots. The tea had been stored in the cellar of David Sutton's house; the site today, 20 Market Lane, is graced with a newer Victorian home. Two doors down from the former Sutton house is the Captain David Mason House (the Dr. Quigley House today). Mason asserted that the tea was burned directly opposite his house in a field. The site is shown on the Pomeroy map of Cumberland County (1862); see p. 5 of this issue. I give thanks to Warren Q. Adams for pointing out our error and providing the details described above.

Tom Kinsella

Patriotic Order Sons of America (P.O.S. of A.) grew out of the Junior Sons of America (J.S. of A.), founded during December 1847 in Pennsylvania to attract young men, ages 16 to 21, and enhance their love of the United States, the stars and stripes, and the nation's founding documents. Dr. Reynell Coates, a member of the Native American Party and candidate for Vice President in 1852, prepared the ritual, the constitution, and authored the preamble for the J.S. of A. He also selected the odes, opening, closing and initiation ceremony, all still in use today. In 1868, this fraternal organization renamed itself the Patriotic Order Sons of America and membership shifted to attract any male above the age of 21. Allentown, Pennsylvania, hosted the First National Convention in March 1872. By 1882, Washington Camps could be found in six other states. Hainesport, New Jersey, had Washington Camp No. 140. Like all fraternal and secret organizations, members were expected to wear their regalia to all meetings. This membership badge and ribbon was produced by the Hyatt Manufacturing Company of Baltimore, Maryland. As indicated by the two images, the member wore the red, white, and blue side for regular meetings and the black side as a sign of mourning when a brother died. The P.O.S. of A. is still an active organization today.

# Our Curiosity with Maps
## and How They Continue to Inspire Us to Create Something New from Something Old

Adam E. Zielinski

What is it about a map that lures the human mind to fix our eyes upon its detailed lines? Why do some of us derive unexpected pleasure from drafting colorful cartographic manuscripts? There is clearly something at work that defies an easy explanation. Is it inherent in our DNA? Is it supernatural? Or is it simply driven by our curiosity to comprehend what we observe? The role of maps in human existence have long played critical roles in advancing civilizations. For millennia, military planners have vied for the most accurate maps of territory and battlefields to gain an advantage over their enemy. Consider the chessboard: does not the checkered-square board serve as a map, revealing strategy as a player moves their pieces into position to strike the opposing player? Or consider a modern television show like HBO's *Game of Thrones*, whose opening credit sequence is a digital map traversing the fictional world's various kingdoms. There's something at play here beyond simply depicting land, water, and cities. We are drawn to them. I believe it's because maps serve as mirrors into the human soul.

First, they are a reminder of where we all are theoretically located at a particular point in time. Whether it's a map of our hometown or a map of some ancient city, we imagine ourselves there, walking around, and gaining knowledge from the territory we survey.

The main purpose of maps is to inform the viewer, and to learn from them. Second, while the development of maps plays the dual role of providing military intelligence and civil planners with structured measurements of city streets, they also serve as windows into world cultures. We pride ourselves on our culture and from whence we came. Some of us enjoy wearing shirts or flying flags as points of pride, while others figuratively beat their chests based on heritage. Maps serve a similar

purpose by declaring to the viewer what 'is' and whether you can identify with it.

Consider why people today hang maps on the walls of their homes. Why do businesses have giant murals of the world's geography in their conference rooms? I myself have three maps of Philadelphia in my dining room. By doing so, I'm declaring that I am somehow identifying with this particular city, and by displaying the city in such a manner, I want visitors to see the city the way I do. I love Philadelphia. It's more than just a place on a map. It's a part of who I am as a person. From the culture to the sports to the iconic people, the attraction is in feeling a connection to something bigger than yourself. And perhaps by its displaying, others too will connect on the same level as I do.

This is my viewpoint, but I could be entirely wrong. If I am incorrect, however, maps would not be found decorating the walls of modern civilization. Google Earth and GPS would not garner the immense popularity they enjoy. Theme parks would discontinue printing them by the millions. Maps are more than just a means of providing us with travel directions. They also instinctively tell us where we've been. In a world often filled with disorder, maps provide order, and thereby provide comfort. Our souls crave it. This is why we stare, and visually comb a map with rare focus. Our curiosity demands we understand it, even if sometimes we fail to grasp its meaning. And as humans, there is something deeply enriching about it.

My research and work on British surveyor and mapmaker John Hills, whose work began during the Revolutionary War, has led me to this place of cartographic intrigue. I have spent three years studying his life and the details that he included in his work. Along the way, as I was rediscovering his remarkable skills as

# The skirmish or [...]
### in the providence of Mount Holly, New Jersey

Count Carl von Donop

von Ewald

skirmish at Petticoat Bridge

VON — 1.

Burlington

von Donop — 2.

Moore's Town

RANCOCA[S]

Griffin Dec 23

In July 1776, forces of Great Britain under the command of General William Howe landed on Staten Island. Over the next several months, Howe's forces, which were British army regulars and auxiliary German troops usually referred to as Hessian, chased General George Washington's Continental army out of New York City and across New Jersey. Washington's army, broken and shedding soldiers from desertions due to poor morale, took refuge in Pennsylvania on the western shore of The Delaware River in November. They removed all the available watercraft to deny the British any opportunity to cross the river.

Howe established a chain of outposts across New Jersey, and ordered his troops into winter quarters. The southern most outposts were located at Trenton and Bordentown. The Trenton outpost was manned by about 1,500 men of a Hessian brigade under the command of Johann Rall, and the Bordentown outpost was manned by Hessians and the British 42nd Regt. contingents, about 2,000 troops in all, under the command of the Hessian Col. Carl von Donop.

Bordentown itself was not large enough to house all of von Donop's force. While he had hoped to quarter some troops even further south at Burlington, where there was strong loyalist support, floating gun batteries from the Pennsylvania Navy threatened the town, and Donop, rather than expose Loyalist allies to their fire, was forced to scatter his troops throughout the surrounding countryside.

As the troops of von Donop and Rall occupied the last outposts, they were often exposed to the actions of rebel raids and the actions of Patriot militia forces that either arose spontaneously or were recruited by army regulars. Those actions frayed the nerves of the troops, as the uncertainty of when and where such attacks would take place, and by what size force, put the men and their commanders on edge, leading them to jump up to investigate every rumored movement. Rall went so far as to order his men to sleep fully dressed like they were on watch.

One militia force that rose in December 1776 was a company under the command of Virginia Col. Samuel Griffin. Griffin was the adjutant to Gen. Israel Putnam, who was responsible for the defense of Philadelphia. Griffin's force, whose exact composition is uncertain, probably included some Virginia artillerymen, Pennsylvania infantry, and New Jersey militia, and numbered five to six hundred. By mid-December, he had reached Moore's Town, about ten miles southwest of Mount Holly.

...he that stands by it now deserves the love and thanks of man and woman. Tyranny, like Hell, is not easily conquered, yet we...

of **Iron Works Hill**

*drafted by: B. Zielinski*

December 21st–24th, 1776, our darkest hour.

SLAB TOWN

Springfield →

Reed

Griffin

By December 21st Griffin had advanced to Mount Holly and established a rough fortification atop a hill near an iron works, south of the Rancocas Creek and the village center. Von Donop sent a Loyalist to investigate, who reported a force of "not above eight hundred, nearly one half boys, and all of them Militia...."

Thomas Stirling, who commanded a contingent of the 42nd positioned about seven miles north of Mount Holly at Blackhorse (present-day Columbus), heard rumors that there were 1,000 rebels at Mount Holly and "2,000 more were in the rear to support them." When von Donop asked Stirling for advice, he replied, "You sir, with the troops at Bordentown, should come here and attack. I am confident we are a match for them."

On December 21st about 600 of Griffin's troops overwhelmed a guard outpost of the 42nd located about one mile south of Black horse at Petticoat Bridge. On the evening of December 22nd Washington's adjutant Joseph Reed, went to Mount Holly and met with Griffin. Reed, who had been discussing a planned attack on Rall's men in Trenton with Washington, wanted to see if Griffin's company could participate in some sort of diversionary attack. Though poorly equipped, Griffin agreed. The following morning, December 23rd, von Donop brought 3,000 troops (the 42nd British (Highland) Regt. and the Hessian Grenadier battalions Block & Linsing) to Petticoat Bridge where they overwhelmed Griffin's men. The Americans retreated to Mount Holly while von Donop reported scattering about 1,000 men near the town's meeting house (off Garden & High Streets). Jäger Capt. Johann Ewald reported that "some 100 men" were posted on a hill "near the church", who "retired quickly" after a few rounds of artillery were fired. Griffin's troops slowly retreated to their fortified position on the hill, where the two sides engaged in ineffectual long-range fire.

Von Donop's forces bivouacked in Mount Holly during the night, where, according to Ewald, they plundered the town, breaking into houses, and getting drunk on stolen alcohol stores. Von Donop himself took quarters in the house that Ewald described as belonging to an "exceedingly beautiful widow of a doctor." Legend has it this woman may have been patriot Betsy Ross. On December 24th they marched to force to drive the Americans from the iron works hill, but Griffin had retreated to Moorestown during the night. For reasons unknown, von Donop decided to remain in Mount Holly, 18 miles and a full day's march from Trenton. By the time he decided to move, a messenger arrived to tell on December 26th, bringing the news that Rall had lost Trenton to Washington that morning.

News and reports of the Battle of Iron Works Hill are conflicting, and precise numbers on the wounded or killed are unknown. Though von Donop's move southward clearly weakened the defenses at Trenton, its claims of Griffin's deception luring von Donop seem to be coincidental as von Donop had already decided to move against Griffin before Reed arrived. However it happened, and the reasons that kept von Donop in Mount Holly on Christmas 1776, American history and George Washington shall always owe a meal of thanks to our hands.

Iron Works
...

a mapmaker, I found an ability within myself to see beyond the lines and the hachure marks and the colors. It wasn't just a map anymore. No, it truly was something much more. And what came next was a payoff I could never have imagined. I found myself sitting down and creating my own maps for the first time. A long dormant talent I had once dabbled in suddenly came roaring back. There is something peaceful about creating art. And isn't that what a map is? A form of art. What do people do at art galleries? Why, they stand and stare, and have the look of a person wrestling with a silent back-and-forth in their mind. It's the allure of thinking beyond yourself and your physical limits. Good art challenges your mind to not just expand your horizons; it challenges you to go beyond the horizon.

With a map, there is a specific dissection of a place in time for our imaginations to fill in what the image cannot do. We then come to the realization that maps are windows into ourselves. They allow us to channel our true nature: discovery through curiosity. All we have to remember is that we can learn something new from something old; even a map made in 1778 has something new to offer with the proper observations. That is what I find enlightening about creating new maps of old events.

Maybe you didn't realize how vital Mount Holly was to the efforts to cross the Delaware and take Trenton in 1776? Maybe you didn't realize that the true story still has life today, and you can contribute to its survival in the memories of Americans. We all have our individual roles to play. Remember, this is *our* story. Time is nothing but a window into ourselves. We can use maps to navigate through its opening.

This map was hand drawn with colored pencils, black felt pens and a geometry ruler and triangle on a standard 18 x 24 inch white drafting paper. I have no professional training in cartography or drafting. I simply like to draw. Succumbing to a tranquil break from the daily grind is not easy for us, and that's why many of us never know what we're truly capable of. While this map may just represent a few passing hours of hobby work, imagine what creative ideas can be channeled with a little time, a little wine, and a healthy pencil sharpener.

## About the Author/Artist

Mr. Zielinski is a historian from Mount Holly, New Jersey. His biography on British surveyor John Hills is currently finding a publisher. He is a published writer with the *Journal of the American Revolution*, as well writing several historical profiles for the American Battlefield Trust's website, where he is a member. He is also a member of the Washington Association of New Jersey, the Mount Vernon Society, The Library Company of Philadelphia, the Historical Society of Pennsylvania, and the Rev War Alliance of Burlington County. He is a graduate of Fairleigh Dickinson University where he studied American history.

## References

"Sketch of Haddonfield, March 1778." Sketch of the roads from Pennyhill to Black Horse through Mount Holly. by John Hills, surveyor, 1778, Library of Congress online. https://www.loc.gov/resource/g3814h.ar125800 /?r=0.406,0.315,0.278,0.138,0.

Hills' map of Mount Holly is particularly useful in examining historic roads through the town. Of interest is the road cited just south of the Rancocas Creek cutting west along Iron Works Hill. Historians have attributed this to being a wagon trail that ran along the creek at the foot of what would become St. Andrews Cemetery. Today, the Battle of Iron Works Hill monument can be found on the overgrown pasture. This map provided the necessary skeletal ingredients for my map of the battle, though I certainly took many liberties to render an original depiction.

"Map of Mount Holly, circa 1876," West Jersey History Project. http://www.westjerseyhistory.org/maps/burlco_ scott_1876_atlas/index28.shtml.

This map provided a useful scale of the streets, creek and layout of the town. Though it is clearly not depicting 1776 township buildings and lands, it provided the necessary dimensions for a blueprint that enriched my battle map for the best accuracy.

The battle map's pictured soldiers, from upper left corner counter clockwise, are Hessian Col. Carl von Donop, Hessian Jaeger Capt. Johann Ewald, a Hessian soldier, a Pennsylvania militiaman, American Col. Samuel Griffin, and American Adj. Gen. Joseph Reed. These were all done from pictures and portraits found online. The text can be attributed to http://www.revolutionarywarnewjersey.com/ new_jersey_revolutionary_war_sites/towns/mount_holly_nj_ revolutionary_war_sites.htm and the *Journal of Capt. Johann Ewald*, which is highly recommended for insight into the British and Hessian movements during 1776 and 1777. His map of Mount Holly was not used for this manuscript. Finally, the text bordering the battle map are portions of Thomas Paine's *The American Crisis*, which was written in the days and weeks leading to the Battle of Iron Works Hill and the surprise attack on Trenton on December 26, 1776.

# Journal of Thomas Hopkins
## of the Friendship Salt Works, New Jersey, 1780

The journal of Thomas Hopkins, preserved at the Historical Society of Pennsylvania, is a fascinating if sometimes frustrating document. It furnishes an abundance of details about the day-to-day operations of a saltworks during the American Revolution and provides intriguing glimpses of rural life in South Jersey. The journal, with its brief, hand-written entries, begins in mid-August and runs through October 1780. Despite the rich detail provided in the 32-page journal, much remains unknown. The exact location of the Friendship Saltworks has not been established, although it was certainly within a few miles of modern-day Absecon in today's Atlantic County. The date of the works' commencement and by whom is unknown. When it ceased operations is also unclear. The trying circumstances under which salt was produced, however, are very clear. Hopkins writes of "shoals of musquetoes" that caused wood cutters to abandon their work, of shortages of provisions that caused the workers to live on fish and clams, of poorly burning green wood, occasional theft, and consistent drunkenness by one of the employees.

Thomas Hopkins, who served as superintendent to the Friendship Salt Works, was born on September 22, 1728, to the unknown wife of Robert Hopkins, although his Philadelphia death certificate indicates his nativity occurred sometime during 1731.[1] Sorting through his genealogy is a challenge since there were at least two Thomas Hopkins in Philadelphia during this period. Born into a Quaker family, he received his education through his father's monthly meeting membership.[2] At some point after reaching his majority, Thomas followed the occupation of his father and presumably his uncle or brother, William, and became a baker.[3,4] As indicated in contemporary advertisements, Robert and William both used slave labor in their bakeries, as did Thomas.[5] Little

is known of Thomas's life prior to the 1750s. On February 10, 1757, he married Sarah Garrigues, daughter of Isaac and Christian Broadgate Garrigues.[6] The Thomas Hopkins Facts webpage in the Garrigues Family Tree indicates that Thomas and Sarah had a son named Isaac, but fails to list any other known children.[7] Based on the journal, clearly they had a son named Robert.

As the American British colonies ran headlong into the fight for independance from the British Crown, all colonists, including Quakers, faced a decision on where they stood vis-á-vis the coming armed conflict. Most Quakers attempted to remain neutral as dictated by their sect's tenets against violence or warfare. Some Quakers, however, aligned themselves with those in rebellion, including Thomas Hopkins. At the June 4, 1776, assembly of the Northern District Friends Monthly Meeting, the following Testimony was read into the minutes:

> Thomas Hopkins of the Northern Liberties of this City, who was Educated & hath made some Religious profession with us, in this time of public commotion had associated with a number of Men, who under a profession of maintaining Civil Liberty; have promoted measures which have a tendency to deprive us of our Religious privileges & oppress many tender Consciences— being very opposite to the principles we profess to the World, which lead them who faithfully adhere thereto, to live in peace & to avoid every kind of oppression. And as it became our concern to treat with the said Thomas Hopkins for his public deviation from our Christian Testimony, & to excite him to grant liberty to a number of slaves he detains in Bondage, which labour has not been attended with the desired effect, he

continuing to advocate his inconsistent conduct. We do therefore testify that he has separated himself from us, until through contrition & a just Sense of his Errors, he becomes willing to acknowledge and condemn them, which we desire he may with the Lord's assistance be enabled to do.[8]

Based on this testimony, it appears Thomas had chosen to eschew the peaceable teachings of his faith and took the American side in the fight for independence. Although no payment vouchers have been identified payable to Hopkins, there is little doubt he baked bread and biscuits for the American troops. The addendum at the end of his journal confirms that Thomas provided provisions and likely baked for prisoners held in Philadelphia after the British took possession of the city. Seeking a long-overdue payment for his work as a victualer among those prisoners, Thomas lamented: "Had I gone to work with my bake houses for the British I could have baked from twenty to thirty hundred of bisquet pr. Day, for which I could have had 7/6, that it would not have been one quarter the fatigue to me as I had with the prissoners...."[9] From this quotation we can infer that Hopkins continued baking during the Revolutionary War, the British occupation of Philadelphia, and while traveling to and managing the Friendship Salt Works in 1780.

Hopkins received some monetary settlement for supplying the prisoners with food during the 1777–1778 British occupation of Philadelphia, but was unhappy with the payment he obtained. He wrote to Robert Morris, Superintendent of Finance, in January 1782. Morris notes in his journal:

> Mr. Thomas Hopkins whose Account was lately settled in the Treasury Office applied to me being unsatisfied with the Settlement. I referred him to Mr Millegan the Comptroller to whom all apeals on the Settlement of Accounts must be made and shewed him the Ordinance to that Effect.[10]

A final entry in Morris's diary for February 22, 1782, reports, "Mr Milligan called with Sundry Papers relative to various Articles of business which I dispatched and returned him the papers and proofs of Mr Thos. Hopkins for farther Consideration...."[11] It is unclear whether Hopkins received the settlement he sought.

At some point, Hopkins entered into a business partnership with his son, Robert, but in March 1786, their bakery partnership ended.[12] By the first half of

1790, Thomas Hopkins had suffered a financial calamity. Under court order, James Ash, Philadelphia County Sheriff, advertised all of Hopkin's real estate for sale.[13] Thomas's son Robert had been swept into his father's economic woes as well.[14] The Philadelphia newspapers of the period provide no further information about the plight of Thomas and his son, Robert.

Hopkins lost his wife, Sarah, to death on May 2, 1816.[15] Like her husband, Sarah endured being separated from the Religious Society of Friends

> ... thro' the inattention to the inward Mentions of Truths, has been seduced by the Enemy of Mankind into the excessive use of strong Drink, also to neglect the attendance of our Religious Meeting, and does not appear convinced of our Righteous Testimony against the practice of Slave Keeping, as she professes an approbation of her Husband's continuing therein....[16]

Thomas Hopkins died on May 23, 1824, at the age of 93; despite his strained relations with the Religious Society of Friends, his remains were interred at the Cherry Street Friends burial.[17]

Many aspects of the journal are of interest to local historians. Hopkins appears to have made the horseback journey from Philadelphia to the New Jersey coast in one day, approximately a fifteen to sixteen hour ride, with rest stops. His usual route was from Philadelphia to Cooper's Ferry, to Haddonfield, to Long a Coming, to the Blue Anchor tavern, to the salt works. Throughout the journal, Hopkins carefully notes exorbitant prices for lodging, board, and ferriage. Today's readers can begin to understand the meaning of the phrase, "not worth a Continental." Depreciation of the American currency was yet another detail of day-to-day life.

The mystery of the journal revolves around the saltworks themselves. Where were they located and how were they financed? A sales advertisement in *The Pennsylvania Gazette*, reproduced at the conclusion of the journal, announces sale of the works on September 26, 1780. The works are located "situate on Great Egg harbour, two miles to the eastward of Absecom bridge."[18] Hopkins's entry for the day of the auction reads, in part:

> Set out for the works where wee arriv'd at two oclock PM where we found L D wife & sister, E B & wife, G Harris, & my son Robt. just going to set down to diner, where wee dined, & the next day the works was set up at Vendue & was bid in for the owners.

L D is Leonard Dorsey, a wealthy Philadelphia grocer who appears to have had a financial interest in the works. E B and G Harris have not been positively identified,[19] and the final clause suggests that the owners, whoever they were, bought back the saltworks. There are intriguing unanswered questions.

The journal has been published twice before: a hundred years ago in slightly abridged form in *The Pennsylvania Magazine of History and Biography*, 42, 1 (1918), 46-61, and in highly abridged form in Ewing and McMullin's *Along Absecon Creek* (Bridgeton, NJ,

1965, 1991). We believe this third transcription, the most complete to date, will be helpful and entertaining to readers. The text has been adjusted in the following ways. Hopkins used minimal punctuation; to improve readability, pointing has been supplied as needed. Hopkins capitalized words frequently but inconsistently; we have regularized his capitalization. His spelling and his abbreviations have been maintained along with his habit of placing final letters of abbreviations in superscript with a nested dash below: we have reproduced this with a period, as thus "2nd."

## The Journal of Thomas Hopkins

Aug.t 11th. 1780
Left home in c.o with James White crossd to Coopers Ferry & p.d ferriage. . . . . . . 24/0/0. Proceeded on the road near to Haddonfield recollected leaving the books behind returnd by my self for them, got them & proceeded back to Haddonfield where I lodgd with J White. Rose the 12th. by day light p.d our reckoning, at Haddonfield . . . . 35/5/0 & proceeded to the Blue Anchor where we fed our horses & got breakfast, rested a little p.d our reck.g 22/10/0. Then sett of* for the works where we arrivd about six oclock through shoals of musquetoes all the way who attackd us on every quarter with great venom. Found one sett of works going, Martin & Nicholas working them, Nicholas Hart hauling wood, about four cord at the works. James Thomas returnd in the evening from the wood cutters & found there was not more than seven or eight cord cut, three wood cutters at work, who came in & said they could not stand it any longer the musquetoes being so very thick. Allen & Young returnd about 8 oclock from Philad.a with eight empty flaxseed casks. Drawd 11 bushells salt this evening.

Sunday Morng Aug.t 13th. 1780
6 oclock weather fair, light breese @ SE. A very fine tide the water very good, opend the gates & filld the pond. The cistern full of excellent water. Went to meet.g with J White & Ja.s Thomas. No body at work except the two men at the fires. In the afternoon very heavy squales with thunder & rain, the evening clear returnd home ab.t 7 oclock. Drawd 11 bushells salt.

Monday Aug.t 14th. 1780
6 oclock wind at SW, fine weather. Martin & Nicholas at the fires. Nicholas Hart halling wood. Jo.s Allen & John

Young getting the waggons in order to go to Philad.a. The woodcutters refus.g to cut induced me to offer them 2/6 p cord, which they agreed to, fearing we should be out of wood & obligd to stop the pans. At ten oclock the tide suiting set the pumps a going but found the sheeting underneath the wheal blown, stopd the wheal immediately lifted it up & J Thomas & I Strickland who was here repair it & set it agoing ab.t 11 oclock. Ab.t dinner time the wind @ NE brisk gale, saw two sail standing to the SE, the one a large schooner the other a brig. After dinner the woodcutters returnd & said they would work no more as the weather was so hot & the musquetoes so thick. Am fearfull unless we can employ some immediately shall be ob.d to stop the works. In the evening Jo.s Allen & John Young set of for Philad.a with 8 teirces† of salt, ab.t one load more in store.

P.d for sundries viz.
Luke Rulong for fish & oysters   17/5/0
1 Gall.n Rum                37/1/0

Deliverd Sundries
Luke Rulong           14 lb flour
John Higbee          129 lb flour in part pay for Hay
Abigail Reed          1 lb Sug on acc.t with GH
[marginalia] Drawd 11 basketts salt.
[marginalia] NB. The eight casks of salt Ja.s White took no receipt for.

---

\* Hopkins invariably spells "off" with one "f."

† Teirce: An old measure of capacity equivalent to one third of a pipe (usually 42 gallons old wine measure, but varying for different commodities; also a cask or vessel holding this quantity, usually of wine, but also of various kinds of provisions or other goods (e.g. beef, pork, salmon, coffee, honey, sugar, tallow, tobacco); also such a cask with its contents (*Oxford English Dictionary*).

Aug.t 15.th 1780.

6 OClock the Morning fine clear but very warm
Martin & Nicholas at the fires as yesterday
& Nicholas Hart Hawling wood, the Wood
Cutters eloped before Day & stole an Ax & a
Loaf of Bread — Draw'd 12 Baskets Salt
Rece'd of Luke Nulong 3 Sheapshead a
8 Doll.s & 12 weak fish a 7/6 —    13 – 10 – 0

5 OClock Clear 16 Morning light breese at
West but very warm Martin & Nicholas
at the fires our wood very Green James
White & Jas. Thomas set off for Philad.a
about 4 OClock PM, like for Rain set
the pump at work Nicholas Hart sick
no wood Halled still Continues very warm
no wood Cutters at work past Nine OClock
the Pickle not boild down yet, Owing
to green wood, the Cistern full of
very good watter

5 OClock 17 Martin & Nicholas at work
Draw'd 12 Baskets Coarse Salt no wind very
warm, Musquetoes & flies plenty; Nicholas
Hart Halling wood; went & Bath'd in Cistern
after Breakfast trim'd Casks, 9 OClock went
& Examined the watter in the ditch & found
it Damed Across so that the watter could not
come up from the bay, then proceded down
to the bay side & tried the watter in the Natturall
ponds & find it very salt ✕ set the Pump to
work; Martin Welson Drunk & very
Abusive

Thomas Hopkins' journal (Am .082/collection 292), Historical Society of Pennsylvania. Journal entries for August 15–17, 1780. Permission to transcribe the journal and to reproduce the page above courtesy of the Historical Society of Pennsylvania. For a digital version of the journal, see https://digitallibrary.hsp.org/index.php/Detail/objects/11183.

Aug^t. 15^th. 1780
6 oclock, the morning fine clear but very warm. Martin & Nicholas at the fires as yesterday & Nicholas Hurt hawling wood, the 3 wood cutters eloped before day & stole an ax & a loaf of bread. Drawd 12 baskets salt. Rece'd of Luke Rulong 3 sheapshead @ 8 doll^s. & 12 weakfish @ 7/6          13–10–0.
[marginalia] N B The three wood cutters chop'd about 2 cords.

Aug^t. 16^th. 1780
5 oclock, clear morning, light breese at W but very warm. Martin & Nicholas at the fires, our wood very green. James White & Ja^s. Thomas set of for Philad^a. about 4 oclock PM. Like for rain, set the pumps at work. Nicholas Hart sick, no wood halled, still continues very warm, no wood cutters at work. Past nine oclock the pickle* not boiled down yet, owing to green wood, the cistern full of very good watter.

Aug^t. 17^th. 1780
5 oclock, Martin & Nicholas at work. Drawd'd 12 baskets coarse salt. No wind, very warm, musquetoes & flies plenty, Nicholas Hart halling wood, went & bath'd in cistern, after breakfast trim'd casks. 9 oclock went & examined the watter in the ditch & found it damed across near the natturall ponds so that the watter could not come up from the bay, then proceded down to the bayside & tried the watter in the natturall ponds & find it very salt. Set the pump to work. Martin Nelson drunk & very abusive.
[marginalia] Return'd from the bay at 11 oclock AM & find it very hott with light air of wind from the S & the tide but indifferent.
[marginalia] Query whether if the natturall ponds was dugg† one spitt deep would it not be great benefit.

Aug^t. 18^th. 1780
5 oclock, clear morning no wind, very warm, musquetoes & flies very plenty. Martin & Nicholas at the fires, agreed with Richard Demey to cut wood at 2/6 apiece or the exchange. Draw'd 10 baskets coarse salt, the wood green. 12 oclock, very hott, looks as if wee should [have] a heavy gust from the NW, goes of again. 3 oclock, fresh

breese @ SW. Sett the pump at work, the tides run low, Nicholas Hart hall'd 3 cords of wood of Ja^s. Weyle cutting, Martin Nelson drunk, left the works from 3 oclock PM until 6 oclock, & I had to go help Nicholas to shift pickle. Jo^s. Allen and Jn^o. Young return'd about 11 oclock @ night from Philad^a. with 8 empty casks. 10 baskets salt.
[marginalia] Martin so very quarelsome with cursing & daming that I could hardly keep my hands of him.

Aug^t. 19^th. 1780
3 oclock, went to the salt house found Nicholas Johnson at work, Martin had not releivd him all night. Sent him to bed, tended untill sun rise, call'd Martin then went & had a fine bathing. Cloudy morning wind @ NW, grows pleasant. Sent Allen & Young to John Higbee for two loads hay, went to the woods with Nicholas Hart found 2 cords & ½ trim'd & lined 10 flaxseed casks they were in very bad order, measur'd up all the salt that was in the store, nine bushells of it was made when I came to the works. Set the pump at work, fill'd the cistern. Draw'd 11 baskets salt. No wood cutters at work this day. The musquetoes & flies exceeding plenty so that I can scarce write, 10 oclock PM.
[marginalia] 11 baskets salt.

August 20^th. 1780
First Day, 6 oclock, fine clear morning wind @ NW, fine & cool. Went & bath'd. Sent Nicholas Hart to see if he could find any more wood, report'd that he found 8 or 10 cords. Went to meeting & in the afternoon made dilegent serch after a house keeper, have some expectation of one to morrow. Nicholas Hart hall'd 4 loads wood, Martin & Nicholas tending fires. Draw'd 10 baskets salt to day.

August 20^th. 1780
Stephen Eyre}
By the recommendation of Hudson Burr, who informed me that thee would be a good hand in the salt house, I take the liberty to write to thee, to know if thee would come & work for us at the Friendship salt works, where wee would give thee good wages & constant employment, should be glad to see thee immediately, or to be inform'd by letter, & in so doing thee will oblidge thy assured friend to serve

Tho^s. Hopkins

August 21^st. 1780
6 oclock, wind @ NW, fine & cool. Nicholas & Martin at the fires, set the pump at work, sent John Young to hall hay from Jn^o. Higby & Joseph Allen to Philad^a. with

---

* The pickle is a strong brine, derived from salt water in evaporating ponds, that is then boiled down in the pans. See William Brownrigg, *Art of Making Common Salt* (London: C. Davis, 1748), readily available on archive.org.

† The journal is damaged here and from "dugg" to the end of the sentence we are following the reading of the 1918 *PMHB* transcription.

five Flaxseed casks salt, cont'g 46 bushells, nine of which I found made when I arriv'd at the works & the eight casks which Jo^s. Allen & Jn^o. Young rece'd the 14 inst. & give no receipt to Ja^s. White for it being in a very great hurry. Tried the watter in the pond & find it ordinary, let it out. Draw'd 11 baskets salt this evening.
[marginalia] NB Jo^s. Allen set of @ 12 oclock AM / 37 buss salt I made.

August 21^st. 1780
Rece'd of Thos. Hopkins five Flaxseed casks salt to be deliverd to L. Dorsey in Philad^a. with 3 ax's to be laid containing 46 busshells.

Joseph Allen

August 22^d. 1780
5 oclock, clear pleasant morning, wind @ west. Martin & Nicholas tending fires, sent Jn^o. Young to hall^g. hay. Went & bath'd at 12 oclock AM. Nicholas Hart return'd from hall^g. wood & broke the little wagon, the large one being broke down before. One oclock opened the gates to get watter but it prov'd bad, let it out again. Sent N Hart with the waggon to N Blackman to be mended, tried to get one but could not. J Young went to hall wood this afternoon. Draw'd 12 baskets salt.
[marginalia] NB Nine busshells this load I found made when I arrived, 37 buss.

August 23^d. 1780
5 oclock, clear still morning. Martin & Nicholas at the fires, John Young hallg wood. Nicholas Hart at work in garden for want of waggon. Stop'd the leaks in the trunk, dug the ditch deper, examined the pumps, stop'd leaks in cistern. 12 oclock PM flies & musqetoes in great plenty, very warm, wind @ west. Tried to set the pump at work, could not fetch it, drawd the 2 boxes found one of the lower box staple draw'd, could not get it riveted this day. Draw'd 12 baskets salt.
[marginalia] J Young 2 load wood this day.

August 24^th. 1780
5 oclock, clear still warm morning. Martin & Nicholas at the fires, Jn^o. Young hall'g wood, N Hart ploughing potatoes, the ground very hard & dry. Set two pumps at work & from tasting of the watter about the pumps I am sure that wee use two much fresh watter & I am of the opinion that if there was a trunk of logs from the ditch across the creek & to have the naturall ponds dug one spitt deep, & to have waste gates from the ditch & pond, that wee should make as much salt in two days as wee do in three. After Breakfast Nich^s. Hart went to cut wood, the waggon not being mended yet. 12 oclock AM, wind @

S, very warm, flies & musquetoes not so bad as yesterday. Good tide [marginalia: 3 oclock] got a pond of good watter. 5 oclock went to wealright after the wagon, he expects to have it done next week. Musquetoes in clouds, enough to eat up horse & foot. Draw'd 10 baskets salt.
[marginalia] NB Broach'd our last barl poark. J Young 3 load wood.

August 25^th. 1780
5 oclock, clear morning, little pleasan[t]. Martin & Nicholas at fires. Went & bought some fresh beef & salted it, set both pumps at work. John Young hall'g wood, Nicholas Hart to cutting wood, having no wagon. Light wind at E 12 oclock AM, very warm, filld the pond this afternoon, having green wood. Draw'd only 10 baskets salt.
[marginalia] J Young 3 load wood.

August 26^th. 1780
5 oclock, cloudy warm morning, light air @ E. Martin & Nicholas at fires, J. Young & Nich^s. Hart hall^g. wood with Jo^s. Allen's wagon. Jo^s. Allen arriv'd here about 6 oclock this morning with 5 empty casks [with] Barney & Henry from Philad^a. Fill'd up 5 casks salt, sett the pumps at work. Taken acc^t. of wood, but about 2 cords left. Barney & Henry employ'd about house to day. Draw'd only 10 baskets salt, the wood was so green.
[marginalia] J Y 4 load.

August 27^th. 1780
First day, 5 oclock, cloudy foggy morning. Martin & Nicholas at fires, our wood green. Set of to go to Little Egg Harbour after hands, paid sixty dolls ferrage. Draw'd only 6 baskets salt.
[marginalia] 60 doll^s.

August 28^th. 1780
Rece'd August 28^th. 1780 of Tho^s. Hopkins five flaxseed casks salt to be deliverd to Leonard Dorsey in Philad^a. containing 45 bushells.

Joseph Allen

2^d day, 6 oclock, clear still morning. Martin & Nicholas at fires. Jo^s. Allen set of for Philad^a. with five casks salt. John Young & Nicholas Hart with him to hall hay from J Read & R^d. Higbee. Barney splitting wood, Henry at work about house, Martin drunk, was oblidg'd to send Barney to tend in his room. Musquetoes not so troublesome. Draw'd 7 baskets salt 4 oclock.
[marginalia] NB Two loads hay one from John Read the other from Rich Higbee. [fitt]ing hoops on 5 casks, 7 baskets.

August 29th. 1780
3d day, 4 oclock, clear still warm morning. Call'd up John
Young to feed his horses. Nicholas Johnson tending
fires. Martin being drunk in the day time was not up
all knight & in the morning went & got more rum,
& because I talk to him about his going on in such
amanner, instead of its having the desired effect, he fell
to cursing & damning, upon which I desired him to go
down to the salt house & mind his business. He told
me that he would go when he pleas'd for that it was
none of my business & fell to cursing of mee. I then
took hold of him by the shoulder & push'd him out of
doors; I told him that if he did not behave better that
I must & would discharge him. J Young & N. Hart
went to hall hay with one team. 12 oclock AM, fresh
breese @ S, got a pond good watter having a full tide,
set 2 pumps at work. Barney splitting wood, Henry in
the house & in the evening Barney & Henry tended in
Martins [unreadable] sent away @ 12 Clock & did not
[unreadable] Draw'd 8 baskets salt in evening.
[marginalia] One load hay from Richd. Higbee & after
hall'd wood & N Hart & my self dug the rase deeper.
Martin Nelson discharg'd this day. 8 baskets.

August 30th. 1780
4th day, 6 oclock, clear cool pleasant morning. Wind at
N, no musquetoes, still a few flies. Nicholas Johnston
& Barney tending. Martin drunk, gone after more rum.
Nichs. Hart splitting wood, wagon not mended yet, John
Young hallg. wood, bot. 47 lb sheepshead @ 15/. Mended
salt house roof. 12 oclock AM wind @ NE. 2 oclock,
heard guns, see two large vessels standg. to S. Good tides
set the pump at work, filld the cistern & pond. Draw'd
10 baskets salt @ 5 oclock PM.
[marginalia] J Y 4 loads wood.

August 31st. 1780
5th day, 5 oclock, rainy night & morning, W @ S. Nichs.
Johnston & Barney tending, N Hart splitting wood,
John Young hallg wood, Henry in house, cooking. 12
oclock AM clear, wind @ SE, full tide, & pond. Nichs.
Hart ploughing potatoes & afterwards, splitting wood. 4
oclock went to N Blackmans after waggon, expect to get
it home tomorrow. Martin Nelson begun to work again.
6 oclock evening in the salt house, the wood very green.
Musquetoes & flies quiet. Draw'd 10 baskets salt @ 12
oclock AM.
[marginalia] J Young 4 loads wood with 3 horses one
being sick of G H's.*

Septr. 1st. 1780
6th day, 5 oclock, cloudy morning wind @ N. Nicholas
Johnston & Martin tending, Nicholas Hart & Barney
splitting wood, John Young hallg wood. 12 oclock AM
wind NE full tide & pond, mended the the watter weal
having two spokes broke & braced it all round, on both
sides, set the pump at work. N Hart got the waggon
home. Henry at work in house having no maid. A day
of rest from musquetoes & flies. J Allen returnd about
9 at night with 2 ½ casks oats. Draw'd 9 baskets salt 12
oclock AM.
[marginalia] J Young 4 load 3 horses one sick of G H's.

September 2d. 1780
7th day, 5 oclock, rainy night & morning. Nicholas &
Martin tending, J Young hallg wood, Nicholas Hart
& Barney splitting, Henry in the house. Boarded the
waggon sides. 12 oclock AM the tide over the meadow,
measured up salt, set the pumps at work. Joseph Allen
did not work this day. No flies nor musquetoes. Small
showers most part of the day, our wood green. Rain'd
often in the night. Draw'd 11 baskets salt 4 oclock.
[marginalia] J Young halld 3 loads with 3 horses.

August† 3d. 1780
First day, 6 oclock, rainy morning, wind at NE blowing
fresh, then shifting to SE with heavy rain, Nichs.
Johnson & Martin tending. 12 oclock AM full tide &
pond, wind NW with fresh breese. Set the pumps at
work this afternoon, filld the cistern so as to run over, our
watter good but our wood very green. Draw'd 10 baskets
salt 5 oclock.

September 4th. 1780
2d day, 4 oclock, clear & pleasant, wind NW. Nicholas
& Martin tending, went to the woods to see if I could
find any wood, found one cord wee being almost out,
sent J Young & Nichs. Hart to hall, Jos. Allen & Barney
splitting, Henry in the house, four hands in the woods to
day. Employ'd in measuring salt & triming casks to send
away to morrow, lined nine casks. Draw'd 11 baskets salt.

September 5th. 1780
3d day, Got up at day break to finish my letter & to set
Nichs. Hart & John Young of for Philada. with nine
flaxseed casks salt containing eighty buss. & ½ which
was all that was made. Nichs. & Martin tending, Joseph
Allen hallg wood, 4 wood cutters at work. Cloudy
morning wind NW. Barney & Henry splitting wood &

---

* See entry for September 24, 1780. G. Harris is mentioned.
The entry suggests that he has an interest in the salt works; the
sick horse may be his.

† Hopkins began to date his September 1 entry as "Au," but
caught his mistake and crossed it out. Here he does not catch
the mistake.

cooking. 12 oclock AM wind NE with showers. Staked and ridered* garden fence this afternoon, rain'd most of the night very fast. Draw'd 9 baskets salt 12 oclock.
[marginalia] Jo^s. Allen hall'd 2 loads wood.

Rece'd 5^th. Sept^r. 1780 of Tho^s. Hopkins four flaxseed casks salt to be delivered to Leonard Dorsey in Philad^a. Containg. 35 ½ buss^s.

his

Nicholas + Hart

mark

Rece'd 5^th. Sept^r. 1780 of Thomas Hopkins five flaxseed casks salt to be deliverd to Leonard Dorsey in Philad^a. containg. 45 buss^s.

John Young

Sept^r. 6^th. 1780
4^th day, 5 oclock, cloudy morning wind NW. Nich^s. & Martin tending, Jo^s. Allen hallg wood, Barney splitting, Henry @ cooking, John London & my self mending salt pan, found seven rivets gone in one place many more elsware. 6 wood cutters at work to day, our wood green. Draw'd 12 baskets salt.
[marginalia] J Allen 4 loads wood.

September 7^th. 1780
5^th day, 5 oclock, cloudy still morning. Nicholas & Martin tending, Jo^s. Allen hallg wood. Sent Ja^s. Whylee to fish & get clams, being out of meat. Three wood cutters in woods, Barney splitting, Henry in house. Set the pump at work, watter ordinary in the pond. At work @ mending the pan. Rain'd very fast in the night. Lived on clams to day. Draw'd 12 baskets salt 2 oclock.
[marginalia] J. Allen 4 load wood.

September 8^th. 1780
6^th day, 5 oclock, cloudy morning wind NW. Nich^s. & Martin tending, Barney splitting, Henry in house. Jo^s. Allen hallg wood, two more cutting wood. Very buzzyly employ'd with Jn^o. London about mending the large pan. 12 oclock AM clear & pleasant no flies nor musquetoes. Set the pump at work. Our wood green, our meat intirely out, lived on clams to day. 10 oclock a beautiful night. Draw'd 11 baskets salt 3 oclock.
[marginalia] J Allen four loads wood.

---

* Construction of a stake and rider fence avoided tiresome digging of post holes. Two crossed stakes formed a crotch upon which rested a horizontal rail, the rider. Multiple stakes were used to support multiple riders.

Sept^r. 9^th. 1780
7^th day, 5 oclock, clear pleasant morning wind @ NW. Nich^s. & Martin tending, Barney splitting, Henry in the house cooking, Jo^s. Allen hallg wood. Finish'd mending large pan & got it in its berth this forenoon, & paid John London, smith, five hundred doll^s. on acc^t. of work done. Set the pump at work 12 oclock AM. Severall applied to cutt wood, expect them next week. Draw'd 11 baskets salt 3 oclock.
[marginalia] Jo^s. Allen 3 loads wood.

September 10^th. 1780
First day, 6 oclock, cloudy still morning light air SW. Nich^s. & Martin tending went to set the pump at work & found head of watter low. Examined the damn & found the trunk very leaky. Went to meeting & in the afternoon made inquirey after beef. The waggon's not return'd yet from Philad^a. Draw'd 11 baskets salt 3 oclock.

September 11^th. 1780
Second day, 5 oclock, clear pleasant morning wind NW. Nich^s. & Martin tending, Barney splitting, Henry in house, Allen hallg wood. Out of meat, went to Jafett Leads & got a sheep, which wee are to give flour for. Sent James Whylee to clam & fish, & wood cutters at work. Nich^s. Hart & John Young return'd from Philad^a. with 5 casks oats, 8 buss^s. went to pay for corn wee borrow'd. Ja^s. Whylee got some fish & about 1500 clams. Draw'd 11 baskets salt.
[marginalia] A smart shower before day. Jo^s. Allen hall'd 3 loads wood, N Hart & J Young got to the works 4 oclock PM, with 5 casks oats.

Sept^r. 12^th. 1780
3^d day, 5 oclock, cloudy still morning. Nich^s. & Martin tending, John Young & Jo^s. Allen hallg wood, Nich^s. Hart to cutting wood. 11 hands cutting wood to day, two of them is Capt Stephens's Negros. Men came this morning fill'd up 5 casks salt to send by J Young. Heavy rain, hail & thunder, most part of the night. Draw'd 11 baskets salt 2 oclock.

September 13^th. 1780
4^th day, Got up about 2 oclock call'd up Henry to get mee breakfast, sent Barney to feed the horse, set of for home 3 oclock through clouds of musquetoes as far as the Blew Anchor, arrived about 10 oclock fed the horse, paid eighteen doll^s., then fed again & arriv'd at Coopers about 6 oclock, paid farrage 8 doll^s. & got home about seven oclock in the evening. Left my son Rob^t. at the works.

September 24th. 1780
Left home in compy. with Jas. White first day about one oclock Septr. 24th. Cross'd to Cooper's paid 20 dolls., proceeded on the road to Long Comeing where wee bated our horses, got a drink & paid our reckoning 24 dolls. [&] set out for Blew Anchor where wee arriv'd in the evening, had our horses fed, got supper, went to bed. Arrose in the morning fed our horses, got breakfast, paid our reckoning 162 dolls. Set out for the works where wee arriv'd at two oclock PM where we found L D wife & sister, E B & wife, G Harris, & my son Robt. just going to set down to diner, where wee dined, & the next day the works was set up at Vendue & was bid in for the owners.

September 27th. 1780
4th day, the 27th got up before day, had our horses fed, breakfasted & set out for home, arriv'd at Blew Anchor at 12 oclock AM,* fed our horses, got dinner, paid our reckoning 54 dolls., then set of at 2 oclock & arriv'd at Cooper's in the Evening, paid my farrage 8 dolls. & cross'd the river & arriv'd at home about 8 oclock.

Rece'd October 11th. 1780 of Thos. Hopkins fourteen hundred & eighteen dolls. & a receipt of Jos. Allen's for one hundred & twenty dolls. which was paid for a pair of shoes for Jos. Allen to David Homen which makes 1600 dolls. in full which I had to take care of for Martin Nelson's

mark<br>
Martin + Nelson<br>
his

October 6th. 1780
Left home October 6th. about 2 oclock PM. Paid ferrage 8 dolls. Cross'd the river to Sam Cooper's, fed my horse with 3 quarts oats & set of at 3 oclock & arriv'd at Murrells, at Long Comeing, where I fed the horse, got supper & went to bed, arose @ five fed the horse paid my reckoning 50 dolls. & got to Blew Anchor, breakfasted & fed my horse with 2 quarts corn, paid reckoning 24 dolls. Stop'd at Sedar Bridge, fed my horse & paid 8 dolls., set of through very heavy rain most of the way & arriv'd at the works at 5 oclock in evening, where I found my son Robt. who inform'd me that one set of works was in blast, & Chas. Mires & Martin Nelson tending, having not more wood hall'd than to keep up the fires until morning when the pickell was boil'd down, draw'd 6 baskets salt. Our wood gone, the watter very fresh, having had a great deal of rain, I concluded it best to stop the works until the watter is better & to get the trunk mended across the ditch.

October the 9th. 1780
2nd day, Morning bot. a bull of Jafett Leads for eight pounds hard money, kill'd him & brought the beef to the works, wheighed about four hundred. Barney halling wood, Henry at work in kitchen, John Young, Richd. Demey & Chas. Mires @ cutting wood, Martin Nelson did not work, yesterday nor to day. Deliver'd to Nehemiah Blackman † lb flour.
[marginalia] Dorsey paid Danl. Leads for the bull eight pounds in full.

October 10th. 1780
3rd day, morning, 6 oclock clear & pleasant, wind @ NW. Barney hallg wood, Martin Nelson began to work to split wood, John Young, Richd. Demey & Chas. Mires cutting, Henry at work in the house. Deliver'd to Jafett Leads ‡ lb flour on acct. of a sheep, & 7 lb flour deliver'd to Jas. Wheyle's wife on acct. of work done.

October 11th. 1780
4th Day, morning, 6 oclock, clear & pleasant, wind N. Barney hallg wood, Martin splitting, Henry in the house cooking, Saml Strickland at work about the trunk. This afternoon two of our horses died with the botts.§ Joseph Allen arrived this evening with one barl. beef & 4 flaxseed casks corn & twenty four hundred Continentall dolls. & Michael Meloney along with him.
[marginalia] Rece'd this day by Jos. Allen 2400 dolls.

October 12th. 1780
5th Day, 6 oclock, cloudy morning wind NE. Barney & Martin employ'd with Saml. Strickland, Abigall Read's Jake began to work to day & worked untill the 18th. for his victuals.

---

† Hopkins left a space for the amount of flour, which was not filled in.

‡ Once again, Hopkins has left a blank space for the amount of flour delivered to Leads.

§ Bots are internal parasites, the larvae of the gasterophilus fly. Unable to survive cold winters, the fly has developed a distinctive strategy for ensuring survival. When a horse licks gasterophilus eggs from its legs, immature larvae burrow into the tissues of its mouth, and when mature are swallowed. Over several weeks they develop into stomach bots, creating deep pits in the stomach and, in serious cases, producing ulcers and perforation. Eventually bots are expelled in the manure, and the cycle starts again.

---

* Here, as in other entries, Hopkins uses 12 AM to denote noon, rather than midnight.

October 13th. 1780
6th day, 6 oclock, foggy morning wind S. Full tide, Jos. Allen hallg wood, Barney & Martin splitting wood, Jake cleaning salt house & pans. John Young left the works this morning without acquainting of me that he was going away & has cutt 5 cords wood & this day Owen Jones & Wm. Tandy came from Jas. Coopers began to cut wood. My son Robt. set of for home after breakfast.

October 14th. 1780
7th day, 6 oclock, clear pleasant morning. Jake @ hallg wood in Joseph Allen's stead, he don't work to day, neither Martin Nelson. Barney hallg gravel on the causeway, Henry in kitchen, four men cutting wood this day & finished stoping the damn & the trunk, Saml. Strickland has worked 4 days this week & Jas. Wheylee employ'd in getting clams.

October 15th. 1780
First day, 6 oclock breakfasted & set out for Little Egg Harbour to get axx's & agreed with Stephen Eyre to come to work in about one or two weeks a[nd] lodged at Moss's.

October 16th. 1780
Second day, morning set off from Moss's & breakfasted at Willis's & had a fateguing walk to the ferry's, paid ferryage seventy dolls. & got to Jafett Leads's, rested little & set of for the works and arriv'd at dusk, having walked near 30 miles. Joseph Allen hallg wood & Barney halling wood & pine notts, Capt Stephens's Luke splitting wood, Martin Nelson idle, & Jake, this day six hands cutting wood. Saml. Strickland employ'd setting the pumps to work by watter.

October 17th. 1780
3rd day, 6 oclock, clear morning, wind at NW. Jos. Allen & Barney halling wood, Capt Stephens's Luke splitting, Henry cooking, Charles Mires, Rich'd Demey, Owen Jones & Wm. Tandy from Jas. Cooper's. Read & Smith cutting wood. Tried the watter in the pond & found it very fresh, let it out, & got a pond of good watter, set one pump at work, & Strickland employ'd in getting the other two fit to work, one of them to have a new lower box, & the other lower box to have a new staple.

October 18th. 1780
4th day, 6 oclock, clear frosty morning, wind NW. Martin & Jake getting ready to light fire. Saml. Strickland got the boxes in the pumps this forenoon. Full tide filld the pond with midling good watter, set the works in blast 10 oclock AM. Joseph Allen &

Barney hallg wood, Luke & Francis Meloney splitting, six hands cutting wood, set 3 pumps at work half after 4 oclock PM. Rebecca Allen came to keep house for us this evening & I spoke to Isaac Cordeary's son about the ditch he was @ cutting from the bay near to the damn. I told him that if he let out the watter I thought he was in a fair way to bring trouble on them & that the owners would sue them damage for every day the works were stopp'd. [He sa]id that he would rather see it [unreadable].

October 19th. 1780
5th day, 4 oclock, clear pleasant moonlight morg. Martin & Jake tending fires, our watter but weak. 6 oclock Jos. Allen & Barney hallg wood, Francis Meloney & Luke splitting, 6 men cutting wood. Set 3 pumps at work, 8 oclock stop'd on acct. of the tide our cistern leakey being empty so long. 12 oclock AM wind SW. Set the pumps to work @ five oclock & shifted pickle for the first time.

October 20th. 1780
6th day, 5 oclock, clear pleasant morning, wind NW. Went to set the pumps to work & found a ditch cut through by the damn so that wee cant pump. Jos. Allen & Barney halling wood & Francis Meloney & Luke splitting, Martin & Jake tending fires, 5 hands cutting wood, Wm. Tandy not well. Din'd & at half after one oclock PM the salt most ready to be draw'd. Set of & arriv'd at Mattox's at 8 oclock night, got up at half after four, had the horse fed. Paid my reckoning forty dolls. & set of at 6 oclock & got to Murrells at Long Comeing @ 8, got breakfast & fed the horse. Paid reckoning 18 dolls., set of @ nine & arriv'd at Joseph Coopers @ one oclock, paid ferrage.

My son Robt left home 24th about noon to go to Burlington, after a horse to take down to the works.

**[End of saltworks journal entries]**

### MISCELLANEOUS ACCOUNT RECORDS AT END OF JOURNAL

Septr. 9th. 1780
Friendship Salt Works To John London Dr.

| | |
|---|---|
| To 360 rivets @ 1d. £1–10 in the old way or exchange @ 90 | 135–0 |
| To two ax's for wood cutters @ 140 dolls. a piece | 105–0 |
| To a coal chizell 9d. or 90 exchange | 3–7–6 |
| To a punch 1/ or 90/ | 4–10– |

To 3 days work at 100 doll^s.                     112–10–
                                            ————————
                                                  360–7–6
Paid
Rece'd five hundred doll^s. of Thos. Hopkins on acct Sept^r.
9^th. 1780
£187–10–              John London

October 7^th. 1780
When I arriv'd at the works after the vendue there was
missing nails, a coal chizell & punch, riveting hammer,
drawing knife, tallow, one tow sheet, a large iron bar, two
sheep skins, one cow hide, one great coat, one pair boots,
one saddle.

Rece'd October 17^th. 1780 of Thomas Hopkins four
hundred & sixty one doll^s. in full.
                                            £172–17–6

October 17^th. 1780
To cash paid John London in full four hundred & sixty
one doll^s.                                 172–17–6

18^th. To cash paid Sam^l. Strickland two hundred dolls.
on acct.                                    75–0–0

11^th. To cash paid Martin Nelson fourteen hundred &
eighty doll^s.

26^th. To 2½ yd^s. tow cloth for Cha^s. Mires @ 30 doll^s. yd.
75 doll^s.                                  28–2–5
Ditto Dr. to a pair wollen trowsers         112–10–
[The two entries above are crossed out and accompanied
by the statement: "Leonard Dorsey paid"]

28^th. To cash paid for a pair overalls three hundred &
twenty doll^s. for John Stewart            120–0–0

Decemb^r. 1781
W^m. Clemons Dr to 7 & ½ cords wood he sold @ 35/
                                            £12–5–0
Ditto C^r. by 4 cords that he cut brought down by Jo^s.
Grice & Reemer
Ditto by 15 cords by
14th Ditto by 17 cords by

## CONCLUDING ENTRY

*The journal concludes with a three-page description of Hopkins's
services to American prisoners in Philadelphia while the city
was occupied by the British, from September 26, 1777 until
June 1778.*

Soon after the British was in possession of Philad^a.
a friend of mine let me know what a distress'd situation
the prisoners were in, that they were without provision
for five days, that they had been seen to pull up the grass
& eat the roots; wee then went & made dilegent search
untill wee had found those that had seen them eat the
roots of the grass. I that afternoon walk'd to Frankford
acquainted Cap^t. Craig of the Light Horse, desired he
would acquaint Genr^l. Washington of their situation
which he told me afterwards he did, that the British
would not admit of any provision to be brought in with
a flag untill Christmas, that from the time that I was
made acquainted with their case, I went to the country
every week & bought provision untill it was sent in by
Excellency, & as I had assisted the prisoners, as soon
as T Franklin was appointed agent, he call'd on me to
know if I would assist him which I did untill Genr^l.
Arnold took possession of the City. Tho^s. Franklin &
my self distributed all the provision & cloathing for
which neither of us rece'd any pay. I took care at diferent
times of 106 head fatt cattle, sold most of the flour,
collected the money, bought cloathing, had it made
& distributed, laid out all my hard cash for cloathing,
firewood & provision before wee had any flour to sell.
Did not receive all my money untill last summer & that
without interest, had I purchased goods for my self it
would have yealded me a good profit. I did buy eleven
hundred buss^s. salt, could have sold it for half Joe Buss^l.
but the Commissary's took it away from us, they said it
was for the use of the armey & when wee where paid
for it, would not buy much more hard cash than the first
cost. I this spring spoke with Ellias Boudinot Commiss^y.
priss^s. to know how I was to be paid for my taking care
of the priss^s. He acquainted me that he had settl'd the
books two years ago with T Franklin, had forgot mee &
all that could be done now was to speak with some of
the members of the Treasury board which he did, & they
are of oppinion that it will be best to apply to Congress.
Now if Congress will be so good as to consider whether
or no my past labour at a time when the distress'd
situation of the unhappy prissoners so loudly call'd for
relief, at a time when the inhabitants of the City was
eyther affraid of the dissorders that was then raging in
jail, of the danger attending it, or of being put into jail
their selves. Had I gone to work with my bake houses
for the British I could have baked from twenty to thirty

hundred of bisquet pr. day, for which I could have had 7/6, that it would not have been one quarter the fatigue to me as I had with the prissoners, besides I should have been look'd upon as a clever fellow, instead of a wicked one, & I am of oppinion from their behaviour they would have been well pleas'd that the prissoners had all died in jail.

## Sale Announcement

"On Tuesday, the 26th instant, will be SOLD by public vendue," *The Pennsylvania Gazette*, September 13, 1780.

On Tuesday, the 26th instant, will be SOLD by public vendue, THE FRIENDSHIP SALT WORKS, situate on Great Egg harbour, two miles to the eastward of Absecom bridge, together with all the buildings, improvements and implements necessary for carrying on the business. The works consist of 8 wrought iron pans, viz. 1 boiler, 22 by 16 feet, 3 ditto, 16 by 22 and half feet, and 4 making pans, 16 by 7 and half feet, all lately set up on a new construction, far superior to any other on the continent; and are capable of making a very considerable quantity of salt, supposed about 100 bushels per day. Also a good dwelling house, salt house, store house and stables, a large covered cistern, 100 feet long, 22 feet wide, and 2 feet deep; the whole erected on a pleasant and healthy point of land. The unexpired term of the lease thereof, and the privilege of cutting wood within one mile of the works, at the moderate price of one bushel of salt for 30 cords of wood, is also for sale. These works are supplied with water from the bay (of the best quality) which is pumped into the cistern by water.

At the same time and place will be also sold, the remainder of the company's stock on hand, consisting of a number of horses and waggons, flour, Indian corn, oats and salt provisions, and a variety of houshold and kitchen furniture, &c. The whole of the works will be sold together or separate as best suit the purchasers. The sale to continue from day to day until the whole are sold.

## Endnotes

1 Utman Family Tree, Thomas Hopkins Facts, Ancestry.com, accessed 3 August 2019.

2 Northern District Friends Monthly Meeting, 1771–1781. Haverford, PA: Haverford College Quaker Collection, June 4, 1776, 211.

3 "To Be Sold by John Lewis," *The Pennsylvania Gazette* (Philadelphia), March 19, 1741, 3.

4 "Philadelphia, June 20, 1758," *The Pennsylvania Gazette*, June 22, 1758, 3.

5 Northern District Friends Monthly Meeting minutes, 1771–1781. Haverford, PA: Haverford College Quaker Collection, June 4, 1776, 211–12.

6 A Record of Friends Certificates of Marriage belonging to the Monthly Meeting of Philadelphia, 1672-1759. Haverford, PA: Haverford College Quaker Collection, 1757, 262.

7 Garrigues Family Tree, Thomas Hopkins Facts, Ancestry.com, accessed 3 August 2019.

8 Northern District Friends Monthly Meeting, 1771–1781. Haverford, PA: Haverford College Quaker Collection, June 4, 1776, 211–12.

9 See final entry in journal.

10 E. James Ferguson, editor, *The Papers of Robert Morris: 1781–1784*, Volume 4, January 11–April 15, 1782 (University of Pittsburgh Press, 1978), 72.

11 Ibid., 291.

12 "The Partnership of Thomas Hopkins & Son." *The Pennsylvania Packet and Daily Advertiser* (Philadelphia), April 8, 1786, 4.

13 "By virtue of a writ of venditioni." *The Pennsylvania Packet and Daily Advertiser* (Philadelphia), June, 4, 1790, 1.

14 "First Notice." *The Pennsylvania Packet and Daily Advertiser* (Philadelphia), June, 30, 1790, 1.

15 Utman Family Tree, Sarah Garrigues Facts, Ancestry.com, accessed 4 August 2019, although the compiler of this family tree fails to provide any evidence for the established date of death.

16 Northern District Friends Monthly Meeting minutes, 1782–1789. Haverford, PA: Haverford College Quaker Collection, February 19, 1782, 6.

17 Philadelphia Monthly Meeting Interment Book, Burial Ground, Fourth & Mulberry, 1820–1840, 23.

18 "On Tuesday, the 26th Instant, Will Be Sold by Public Vendue," *The Pennsylvania Gazette* (Philadelphia), September 13, 1780.

19 G Harris may be George Harris, born in Burlington, New Jersey but moved to Philadelphia in 1769. He married out of unity with the Friends in 1774 and the Society disowned him in 1777 for wartime activities. EB could be Everard Bolton, a Quaker shopkeeper in Philadelphia. His brother, Samuel, married a Scull from Egg Harbor, which might link Everard to the salt works.

# The New Old Cedar Bridge Tavern

Jessica Chamberlain

Cedar Bridge Tavern, carefully restored as a historic site and interpretive center, held its grand re-opening on April 1, 2019, approximately two hundred years after the current tavern was erected. Built circa 1816, the tavern is the second public house on the site, the first dating to circa 1743. The Cedar Bridge Tavern site holds historic significance as the reputed location of the final skirmish of the American Revolutionary War (more on that later), yet the focus of the restored tavern and interpretive center is not a single time period or event, but rather the entire span of service of taverns at this location. Located in rural Barnegat Township, the tavern and associated five acres have been lovingly preserved by the Ocean County Parks Department (and its partners). Because of its remote location, it is far too easy to bypass the tavern even if driving close by on the surrounding roads. We hope that the traveling public make it a priority to turn down the dusty, gravel road leading to the tavern. If you do, you will be rewarded with a fascinating visit to a bygone past.

Restoration and renovation of the tavern site began in 2012, when Ocean County gained full control of the property. The county undertook extensive site studies and planning, retained preservation specialists with a range of expertise, and engaged architects and builders with the goal of stabilizing the structure but also uncovering and displaying the details of its long history as a tavern and, in some periods, a private dwelling. Visitors will encounter timelines and maps that detail the owners of the tavern as well as its prominent identification on various eighteenth-century and nineteenth-century maps.

In the main dining room, visitors will find a replicated tavern setting alongside the oldest bar in New Jersey—and possibly in America. Disclaimer: alcohol is no longer served. The history of each room is visually presented through artifacts and furniture: cups, bowls, dishes, tables and chairs. Paintings depict multiple points in history. One upstairs room serves as a gallery of photographs of Revolutionary War sites, many not far from the tavern itself. You can walk into a typical tavern sleeping quarters—

Cedar Bridge Tavern, April 8, 2019, one week after its grand re-opening.

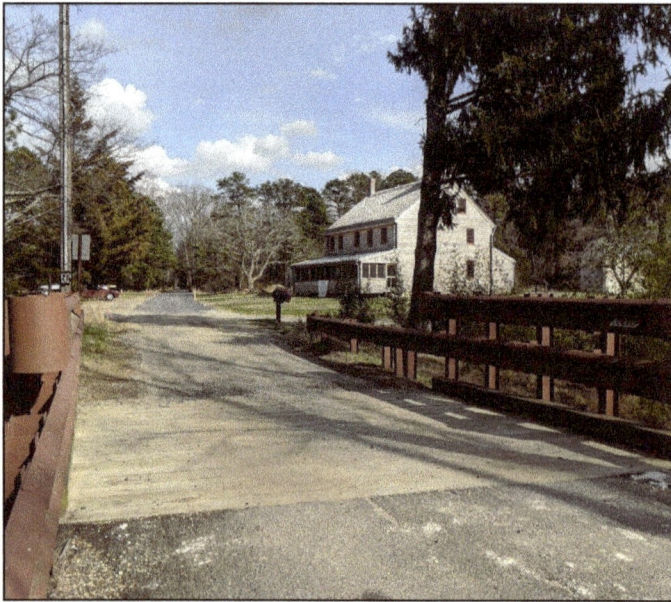

View of the tavern from the current bridge. This may have been the approximate location of the skirmish which took place on December 27, 1782.

## CEDAR BRIDGE TAVERN OVER TIME

c. 1816

c. 1830

1938

c. 1979

2018

The evolution of Cedar Bridge Tavern's structure over time.

Reproductions of contemporary drinking ware on shelf behind the oldest extant bar in New Jersey.

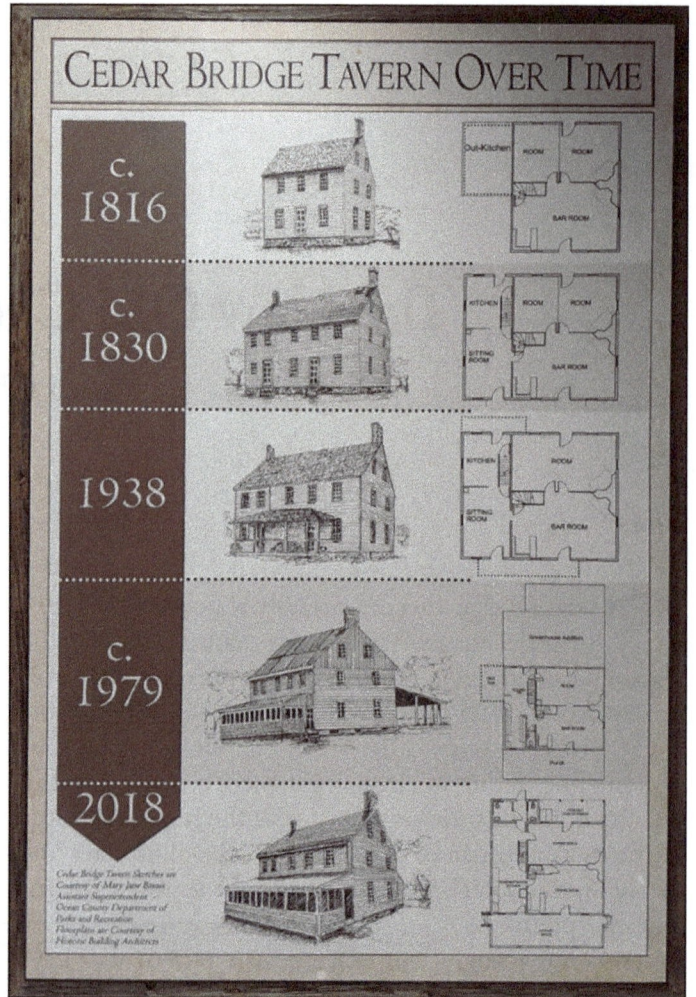

"Affair at Cedar Bridge," painted by Louis Glanzman. On display at the tavern.

with straw filled mattresses, travelling trunks, and night vessels. Visitors can also enjoy pre-recorded videos explaining various physical or historic aspects of the tavern.

Most impressive about the Cedar Bridge Tavern site is the preservation of the stories about its many owners and guests across the span of its existence. Visitors will learn about Captain John Bacon, the notorious loyalist whose presence precipitated "The Affair at Cedar Bridge." On December 27, 1782, New Jersey militia Captains Richard Shreve and Edward Thomas led a party of patriots against Bacon and his loyalist band at "Cedar Creek Bridge." After a heated exchange of gunfire, in which one patriot and one loyalist were killed, the wounded Bacon and his men escaped. Visitors will also learn about John and Elizabeth Wildermuth, tavern keepers, and for a time owners in the 1840s and 1850s; and Rudolph "Rudy" Koenig, the final owner who sold the site in 2007 to Ocean County, retaining use until his death in 2012.

Koenig, who purchased the property in 1959 and used it as his home, is credited with preserving the tavern in the second half of the twentieth century, until the county purchased it. His presence safeguarded the site

The mailbox of Rudolph Koenig, the last private owner of the Cedar Bridge Tavern.

from vandalism and arson, the fate of so many other Pine Barrens historic sites. Koenig was a larger than life character. He moved to the tavern when nearby sleepy Tuckerton became "too big for him." A handyman of sorts with experience as an electrical linesman, Rudy lived the life of an eccentric rural bachelor, installing a jacuzzi and sauna in the tavern, using a boat as goldfish pond, and owning two buses that he never drove. Learning his story alone makes a visit to the tavern fulfilling.

On the day of my visit, Michael Mangum, Tim Hart, and Lucas DiMartini provided the tour. Each is deeply knowledgeable about the history of the tavern and the many fascinating details of its restoration, but as a group, they are also focused on the future. They know that the side trip down the dirt road offers insight into the history of the Pine Barrens and ways of life now largely forgotten. They are working to expand the tavern's use as a destination for school children, inquisitive families, nature and history lovers. In the past, the tavern was a stopping off place for most guests, not a *destination*. Today and in the future, given the excellent work of Ocean County, it *is* a destination—one that allows visitors to educate themselves while simultaneously appreciating their own local history.

The Cedar Bridge Tavern is located on 200 Old Halfway Road, Barnegat, NJ, 08005. It is easily accessible from Route 72 or from the Garden State Parkway (exits 58 and 63). The Tavern is currently open every day until 4 p.m. except Wednesday. Weekdays open at 8:30 and Weekends at 10 a.m. The ceremony commemorating the skirmish will be December 15 at 1 p.m. For more information call (732) 929–4769.

## About the Author

Jessica Chamberlain is a Literature major at Stockton University. She grew up in Old Bridge, New Jersey, and chose Stockton to indulge herself in the history of South Jersey. Her favorite works of literature are those written by Octavia Butler as well as any novels written in or about the Victorian Era. In her free time, she enjoys painting as well as watching her favorite television series "It's Always Sunny in Philadelphia." After graduating in May of 2020, Jessica hopes to work as an editor.

YACHTING ON BARNEGAT BAY, N.J.

Postcard of yachting on Barnegat Bay, from a glass negative. In the early 1970s, my family was gifted with a box of seventeen glass negatives dating from around 1910. They were in surprisingly good shape, although, to our dismay, a few broken ones had been discarded before we received them. At the turn of the twentieth century, Joseph Gaskill served as Waretown's postmaster and the proprietor of an ice-cream and candy store on the Old Main Shore Road. He commissioned the glass negatives from Howell photographer Alick Merriman as a set of "real photo" Waretown postcards. They were sold in his store, Gaskill's Emporium. From the arrival of the railroad in 1873 until the World War II era, Waretown was well known as a vacation spot for hunters and fishermen. Tourists were guided to prime spots by Waretown's many sea captains, retired from the coasting trade. This postcard of sailboats came from a glass negative with a broken corner, fully restored by the magic of today's digital software.

# A Window to the Past:
## Waretown's Glass Negative Postcard Set

Adele R. Shaw

One day, over forty years ago, a man and a woman visited my parents. I was about twelve years old at the time, and they were complete strangers to me. The woman held a small box, the lid printed with holly and Christmas candles, even though it was summertime.

Intrigued, I lingered as the adults gathered in the parlor. The woman turned out to be a distant cousin of my mother's. She explained, "We are getting ready to sell the house in Waretown, and emptying the attic. I came across these old glass negatives, and thought you would like to have them, since you are the last of the family in Waretown."

Setting the box on her lap, the lady carefully lifted the lid, and took out a thin pane of glass. It was nothing like the strips of tiny plastic negatives that came from my father's camera. I had never seen anything quite like it. She held up a five by seven-inch rectangle, tinted black and white, with the lights and darks reversed. When she held it to the light, Waretown's long ago one-room schoolhouse leapt to life—the sweet old school that had been torn down just a few years before. But the building looked different than I recalled. Children stood outside, dressed like characters from *Little House on the Prairie*. I leaned forward for a closer look. Seeing my interest, she handed the negative to me.

With trembling fingers, I lifted it to the light, so my parents could also see. The little glass pane was a window back in time. I was gazing through a portal to Waretown's past.

My mother explained, "My Great-Aunt Annie was Joe Gaskill's second wife. They owned a candy store and ice cream parlor on Main Street called Gaskill's Emporium. They also ran a horse-drawn taxi service from the house. When I was a kid, it was a real treat to walk over there and get ice cream."

The lady nodded. "These glass negatives were postcards they had made to sell in the store. I am not sure when they were taken. I threw out the broken ones."

Dad's head shot up. "Do you still have the pieces? I would gladly glue them back together."

The lady nodded sadly. "No, I'm sorry. I never thought of that. They went out for the trash yesterday."

My heart sank. There had been more glimpses through the veil, reflections we would never see.

Even then, as a child, I had always loved and felt drawn to the past. My mother's stories of growing up in Waretown back in the twenties and thirties made me long for that lost world, convinced that I had somehow been born in the wrong time.

But here, now, in my fingertips, was the most incredible time capsule I had ever seen. Within the box were sixteen other glass negatives—literally a walk down Main Street in the early twentieth century.

In 1979, a few years after we received the glass negatives, my parents hosted Erik Wünsche, a Swedish exchange student, for a year. He went to Southern Regional High School, and designed a photography project around the glass negatives. Working with his teacher, he developed them all and matted the prints.

These negatives and the accompanying prints became treasured family heirlooms, and I set out to learn all I could about the scenes they portrayed. My interest in local history eventually led me to become President and Historian of Waretown Historical Society.

So, travel back in time with me to the Waretown of a century ago. Let's stroll together down Main Street on Woolman's 1877 survey map,[1] as the old postcards from the attic of Gaskill's Emporium bring the time and place to life.

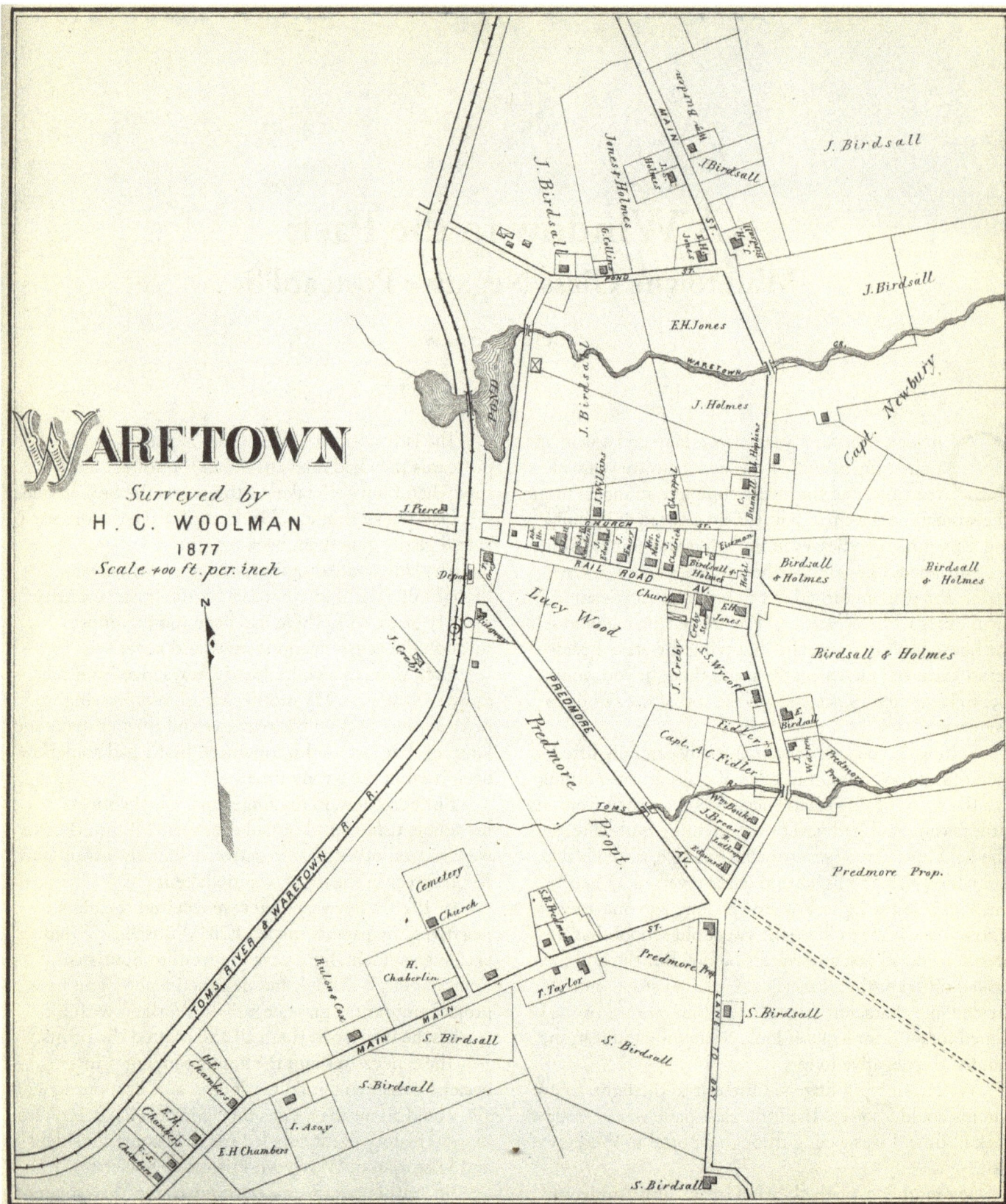

"Waretown," *Historical and Biographical Atlas of the New Jersey Coast* (Philadelphia: Woolman and Rose, 1878). Courtesy of Special Collections & Archives, Bjork Library, Stockton University.

## A Window to the Past

Alick Merriman, a photographer from Howell, New Jersey, made these postcard photos sometime in the first decade of the twentieth century. A series of dating clues, which I will share as we go along, makes clear that they must have been taken between 1895 and 1914. Merriman was well known at the time for "real photographs" of the pinelands and Jersey Shore; what we know of his career suggests a date c. 1910 for these images.

This spot was Waretown's town center in the late Victorian Era. Red Men's Hall, built in 1850, is the plainer building next to the Emporium's fancy porch. The township committee met at the hall, and it housed the first meeting of Waretown Fire Company. But it is best known as the home of Red Men Tribe Chickasaw 113, and their ladies, the Order of Pocahontas.

The Red Men claim their roots from the Sons of Liberty, who dressed as Native Americans for the Boston Tea Party. Their dues funded disability and death benefits, in the days before health insurance.

Below is the club regalia of William Birdsall Wilkins, Waretown's Brick and stone mason. He also belonged to the Jr. Order of the United American Mechanics, another club that met at the hall. Their Ladies were called the Daughters of Liberty. Ware Council was named for Abraham Ware (originally spelled Waier), who built a gristmill here in 1739. The little town that grew around it was first known as Ware's Mill, and then Waretown, in his honor.

The two buildings still stand side by side, although now as private

Merriman postcard of Shore Road, Waretown, from a glass negative. This photograph reveals two of the busiest places in town: Gaskill's Emporium and Red Men's Hall. The Emporium is the building with the extended porch roof. It was an ice cream and candy store that also provided horse-drawn taxi service, and served as the Post Office until 1914. The plainer building next door is Red Men's Hall. Built in 1850, the hall was a meeting place for Waretown's many lodges and ladies auxiliaries in that social age before television. Both buildings remain standing today.

Notice the black band across the bottom right of this photograph. When you see that little black band, you know the image was originally a Merriman postcard.

In this photograph, we are standing at the intersection of Main and Chapel streets, coming up on Warren's Bridge at the bend in the road. Back then, Main Street was known as the Old Main Shore Road, or the New York Road, as it ran from New York to Cape May.

Route 9 was built in 1925 when they straightened the old road for Model T's. Today, Waretown's Main Street is actually a forgotten twist of the Old Main Shore Road, cut off when the highway was straightened. The postcard shows Gaskill's Emporium on the right, with its extended porch roof. A gas lamp with a white pole stands in front. That lamp is a dating clue—the gas line came down Main Street in 1895.

(Left) "Ware Council" silk flag and Jr. O.U.A.M. club badge. (Right) Ribbon from Chickasaw Tribe. These relics from clubs that met in Red Men's Hall belonged to Waretown's brick and stone mason, William Birdsall Wilkins 1852–1932. Courtesy of the Waretown Historical Society.

Merriman postcard of Gaskill's Emporium when it housed the Waretown Post Office. Note the horse-drawn taxi on the left side. Unfortunately, no glass negative of this print exists. Courtesy of the Waretown Historical Society.

homes. A later owner of Red Men's Hall found a child's coffin in the attic, to his surprise and consternation. An older resident solved the mystery by recalling that the coffin was used in an initiation ceremony, illustrating "dust to dust."[2]

Above is a closer look at Gaskill's Emporium, with the horse-drawn taxi out front. This photograph is not from the glass set, but another old Merriman postcard donated to the Historical Society. Perhaps it originated from one of the broken negatives.

The men have not been identified. One may be Joe Gaskill himself. The fact that this photograph is labeled "Post Office" is another dating clue. It must have been taken prior to 1914. That year, Pearl Bonnell became postmaster, and the post office moved from Gaskill's Emporium to the general store at 55 Main Street. Twice a day, at 6:00 a.m. and 8:00 a.m., Waretown's postmaster went to the train station and picked up the mail. At the time, the town had 16 lock boxes and 16 call boxes.[3]

To the right is a photograph of Annie Gaskill as a young woman, my mother's great-aunt. Annie married Joseph Gaskill sometime after the death of her first husband, Noah Headley, in 1913. Joseph Gaskill's first wife, Josephine, had died in 1909. The 1920 and 1930 census records show Joseph and Annie as married and running an ice cream and candy shop in Waretown. Annie is the lady we have to thank for saving the glass negatives, so many years ago.

Continuing north along the Old Main Shore Road, we approach Warren's Bridge over Tow's Creek, at the

bend in the road. In the Warren's Bridge postcard, which appears on the following page, we clearly see two houses. At the center is the Warren Homestead, and the one to the left was owned by Captain Ezekiel Birdsall. Ezekiel owned the ship MAGELLAN, sailing out of Waretown in 1853.

The Warren family name goes back around here for many generations. Captain Joshua Warren, in his schooner MARIA, was among the local mariners harassed by the British during the War of 1812. During that conflict, Britain blockaded our coast, attempting to starve the populace into submission. Many American vessels were captured, and then either confiscated or burned. The village of Warren Grove was named for Joshua Warren.[4] This house belonged to Joshua's son John, and John's sons William and George. All were sea captains, even Joshua's great-grandson, Paul Warren.

The Warren house is no longer standing. It has been replaced by a modern home. The Ezekiel Birdsall house, however, still looks much the same as in the postcard.[5]

Annie Smith Headley Gaskill, 1871–1934. After Joseph Gaskill's death, his second wife Annie saved the glass negatives from the postcard set. They were eventually passed down through her family. Photograph courtesy of the author.

By 1860, Captain John Warren sailed several vessels out of Waretown Harbor: MODEL, ONEIDA, and the SARAH AUGUSTA. He also served as keeper of Barnegat Lighthouse. Nicknamed "Old Barney," this famous guardian of Barnegat Inlet was commissioned in 1859, replacing a smaller, dimmer light from 1834. The Merriman lighthouse postcard contains another unique dating clue: The keeper's house. This beautiful home was built in 1893, as a "triplex," housing the families of the Keeper and his two assistants. It was destroyed by a storm in 1920,[6] proving the postcards were made before that date.

The Lighthouse Keeper was required to have two assistants, because someone needed to be on the lantern platform at all times from dusk until dawn. Barnegat Light was assigned a swivel beacon. The exact ten second interval between each flash had to be maintained, so mariners could identify it from out to sea in the dark. The beam could be seen for twenty miles.[6] The tower was painted red and white for daytime identification. This was very important, as 200 ships *a day* passed the inlet back then, and the parade of sails continued all night long.

As lighthouse keeper, John Warren had many responsibilities. Inside the tower stands a cast iron spiral stairway of 217 steps. The narrow end of each step is attached to a large iron pipe stretching from the base to the lantern platform. This pipe housed the cords and weights that made the

Merriman postcard of Warren's Bridge in Waretown from a glass negative. The bridge crosses Tow's Creek. The houses belonged to sailing ship captains from generations of Waretown seafaring families. Left, Captain Ezekiel Birdsall, and right, Captain John Warren. Only the Birdsall house remains standing today.

Merriman postcard of Barnegat Light House from a glass negative. It clearly shows Barnegat Inlet, with today's Island Beach State Park on the left. Note the keeper's house: it was destroyed by a storm in 1920. In 1876, Waretown and Brookville joined together to become the Township of Ocean. We took that name because our boundaries literally sail across the bay and through the inlet, just as our old sea captains once did.

lens revolve. "Winding the lens" was a huge task. It was like winding a giant cuckoo clock, only the weights were more than 150 pounds and the cords were over 100 feet long.

The keepers were required to wind the lens *every hour* between sunset and sunrise, to maintain that ten seconds of darkness between each flash. "While one keeper wound the mechanism, another stood on the platform, turning the lens by hand, keeping the proper interval."[6]

When high winds swayed the tower, the mechanism would not work. That meant that in the worst weather, during gales and hurricanes, the keepers had to turn the lens manually, sometimes all night long.

Whale oil was preferred for the lamp, as it burned with a bright, clear light. All the oil to keep the lamp aflame had to be carried upstairs. A five-gallon can was always at the bottom of the stairway, ready to be grabbed by anybody going to the top. Cold weather congealed the oil, so the keeper had to warm it before use.[9]

Now we have arrived at the intersection of Main Street and today's Bryant Road, listed here by its name on the Woolman map: Bay Road. This scene is deeply

I thank my friends for their patronage of last year, and will continue to supply them with Ice Cream, Confectionery and Fruits. Liberal terms made with Churches and Societies.

**J. W. LETTS,**
Waretown,    New Jersey.

authentic; there is even horse manure in the middle of the street. My dad was born in 1919. As a boy, it was his chore to run out, shovel that up, and put it on the tomato plants. He hated that job.

Letts store stands on the corner, facing the camera. John Wesley Letts owned the store when this photograph was taken. It was Waretown's post office prior to Gaskill's emporium, with J. W. Letts' sons serving as postmasters. Perhaps they are the ones in front of the building. Note the gas lamp. Above is an April 1895 advertisement from the *NJ Courier* for the store.

Merriman postcard of Bay Road in Waretown from a glass negative. The building facing the camera is Letts Store, which served as Waretown's Post Office prior to Gaskill's Emporium. The building became known as Goff's Store sometime after J. W. Letts' sudden death in 1911. It is now a private home.

Sometime after J. W. Letts' death in 1911, the building became known as Goff's store. There is an old family story that J. W. Letts went out in his horse-drawn wagon to cut firewood. A few hours later, the horse brought him home, dead in the back. Records say he died of "Apoplexy," the old name for a stroke.

J. W. Letts also owned Letts farm, and sold vegetables to the Campbell's Soup company. He served as a township committeeman. He was also a Civil War Veteran, enlisting with the Twenty-third New Jersey Volunteers. Letts Landing Road in Waretown was named for him. His house still stands, not far from where Letts Landing merges with today's Lighthouse Drive. Letts Farm is now the Holiday Harbor development, and Letts Store is a private home.

Merriman postcard of the Atlantic House, Waretown, from a glass negative. The Atlantic House was a guest house for hunting and fishing tourists run by Captain Thomas Stackhouse, after retirement from the sea. His son Leon inherited his father's yacht, the GENEVA, and continued the operation for many years afterwards.

Continuing west at the intersection, just behind Letts Store, Bay Road became Railroad Avenue on the Woolman map. We have now arrived at another landmark of Victorian Waretown—Captain Tom Stackhouse's Atlantic House.

As the age of sail ended, many of our sea captains re-invented themselves as hunting and fishing guides for tourists from Philadelphia and New York. From the arrival of the railroad in 1873 until the World War II era, Waretown was a high-class tourist destination.

Captain Tom Stackhouse was born in 1861. At twelve, he became apprenticed to another Waretown sea captain from the Main Shore Road, Captain William Burden. They shipped lumber and oysters on the schooner EVA HOLMES. Both survived the shipwreck in 1884 when EVA HOLMES went down off the coast of Maryland. The story even made the *New York Times*: "The schooner was caught in a heavy gale and labored so heavily that she sprang a leak. The crew was unable to free the hold, and the leak gained until the schooner was in a sinking condition." Miraculously, the crew was rescued by a passing ship and dropped off in New York. Together, Captain Burden and Tom Stackhouse walked all the way back to Waretown.[10]

Later, Captain Stackhouse was master of the schooner GEORGE P. HALLOCK. He made frequent trips around Cape Horn to San Francisco, long before the Panama Canal cut the voyage in half.

As the age of sail gave way to engines, Captain Stackhouse would not switch. He said, "No sight equals that of a ship under full sail—it makes a fellow think he must be up and going."[11] He continued into his seventies, when he turned the GENEVA over to his son, Leon, who became a trusted guide in his own right.

Captain Thomas Stackhouse 1861–1933, at the helm of his yacht GENEVA. Photograph courtesy of Waretown Historical Society.

Merriman postcard of Waretown Methodist Church from a glass negative. Note the classic Ford Model S Roadster parked out front. The church was built in 1850, and a parsonage was built next to it in 1912, on the lot behind the car. Waretown's congregation eventually outgrew the little church, so a larger one was built across the street in 1968. The old church was torn down in 1972, but the parsonage remains standing. It is still used by Methodist ministers and their families.

Unfortunately, the Atlantic House is no longer standing. The spot today is a parking lot for Waretown Methodist Church.

Right next to the Atlantic House on Railroad Avenue stood Waretown Methodist Church (above). I believe the car is a Ford model S roadster, introduced in 1907. I do not know the identity of the young man, although he carries himself like the car's proud owner.

I do know that the Birdsall family donated the land upon which the Waretown Methodist church was built. They created a family fortune in the coasting trade by building and sailing two and three-masted schooners. The coasting trade was much like today's trucking industry, moving oysters, clams, lumber and charcoal up and down the eastern seaboard. If anybody could afford a classy ride like that, it would be one of the Birdsalls.

Here is another postcard dating clue—a parsonage would be built for Waretown Methodist Church in 1912. It would rise on the lot behind the car, where the trees are, to the left in the photograph.

Interior of Waretown Methodist Church, with gas lights. This photograph of the old church was probably taken on Easter Sunday. Photograph courtesy of Waretown Historical Society.

On a personal note, my grandparents, Ida Wilkins and Fred Letts, met at a church picnic at Waretown Methodist Church. They were married on January 11, 1914, around the time this photograph was taken.

For the record, Church Street on the Woolman map was *not* named for this church, but for a small Universalist Chapel, which still stands as a private home today.

Waretown Methodist Church was built in 1850. Back then, it was known as the Methodist-Episcopal Church. By 1893, the building needed repairs. A belfry was added, and the entry vestibule turned to face north, as it appears in the postcard. The carpenters salvaged wood from a wrecked sailing ship on the bayfront to keep costs down. Pitman Camburn carried timbers from the wreck to the church site on his back.[12]

Although not a postcard, the photograph on the previous page provides a good view of the church's interior, showing its recessed pulpit. It was lit first by kerosene, and then gaslights, and finally electricity. The lighting in the picture appears to be gas, judging by the pipes descending from the ceiling. The original pulpit and ornate preacher's chairs now belong to Waretown Historical Society.

By the 1960s, Waretown outgrew the little church, and it needed extensive repairs. The new Waretown Methodist Church was built across the street in 1968. It will always be the "new" church to those of us who knew and loved the old one.

In 1972, the old church was torn down. However, the bell from its unique little belfry was mounted in the sign in front of the new church. Today, the parsonage is the only structure that remains. A small, grassy lot on one side recalls where the old church once stood, and the parking lot on the other side recalls the Atlantic House.

Losing so many Waretown landmarks within a few years of each other was a sad end to an era. Voices at the time cried, "Progress! Out with the old—in with the new!" I

still wish those wonderful old buildings could have been preserved somehow, that things could have been different. John Greenleaf Whittier's words from 1856 still ring true: "Of all sad words of tongue or pen, the saddest are these: 'It might have been.'"

Continuing down Main Street, we see another Birdsall house and farm. Interestingly, the "Magic Yeast" sign on the telegraph pole to the left of the postcard reveals another dating clue. According to the Smithsonian's National Museum of American History, this product was manufactured between 1886 and 1929.

This lovely old Victorian was built by Jacob Howard Birdsall. The eighth child of Jacob and Rhoda Birdsall, he was born in Waretown in 1839. He attended school here, then went to sea at fifteen and learned navigation. In just five years, he owned not only the schooner he commanded, but interest in two more. During the Civil War, his large personal fleet was chartered by the Federal Government.[13]

In 1865, Jacob Howard Birdsall married Emeline Holmes. They had four children. He built his beautiful farmhouse with a widow's walk so Emeline could watch for his vessels in Waretown Harbor. Jacob Howard Birdsall made his fortune and retired from the sea at 45.

BIRDSALL HOUSE. WARETOWN, N.J. 4

Merriman postcard of the Captain Jacob Howard Birdsall House, Waretown, from a glass negative. Jacob Howard Birdsall was part of a dynasty of Waretown Sea Captains, amassing great wealth from the coasting trade. This house was built beside Waretown Creek, on the bay meadows along the Old Main Shore Road. On moving to Florida, Jacob Howard Birdsall sold his Victorian gingerbread mansion to another retired sea captain, who named it the Acacia House, and provided bed and breakfast lodgings for the tourist trade. Later, it belonged to the Corliss family. Unfortunately, the house was torn down by the developers of Skippers' Cove in the early 1960s. Waretown Library is on the spot today.

(Left) Jacob Howard Birdsall 1839–1919. (Right) Amos Birdsall 1829–1909. Both Birdsall brothers were born and raised in Waretown, the offspring of generations of sea captains. The brothers owned fleets of schooners that moved charcoal, clams, oysters, and lumber up and down the eastern seaboard. This was called the coasting trade. Photographs courtesy of the Ocean County Historical Society.

Then, he served as an Ocean County Freeholder from 1890–1899.[14]

The Birdsalls formed the backbone of Waretown's population for nearly a century, intermarrying with other old seafaring families like the Newburys, the Falkenburghs, and the Holmes. These families formed Waretown's high society back in the day, with their big, stately homes, tall ships in the bay, and acreage of property on the Main Shore Road. Whispers of their wealth and prestige linger at the old cemeteries. Look for the biggest, most ornate monuments—chances are good they belong to a sea captain and his family.

The Birdsalls were Quakers, arriving in the area around 1732, a few years before Abraham Waier and his gristmill.[15] Their men built and sailed two and three-masted schooners, where Waretown creek empties into Barnegat Bay. Waretown Creek is to the right of Jacob Howard Birdsall's house, just outside of the photo. The spot was called Shipyard Point, and located approximately where Long Key Marina is now.

By the turn of the twentieth century, the Birdsalls were among the richest men in Ocean County.[16] Above

THE CEDARS. WARETOWN N.J.

Merriman postcard of the Cedars, Waretown, from a glass negative. It is unknown if this house was remodeled, or is no longer standing. It was probably a guest lodge at the time of the photograph, judging from the name.

are photographs of Jacob Howard Birdsall, and his brother, Amos, from Ocean County Historical Society.

Amos left school at twelve to follow the sea. He started his career in the coasting trade by sailing to New York City, then branched out to Virginia, the West Indies, and the Gulf Coast of Mexico. He became "one of the most remarkably prosperous coastal traders," building the earliest known six-masted schooner.[17] After retirement, Amos Birdsall was the second president of the First National bank of Toms River,[18] which, after a series of mergers, is now part of Wells Fargo.

These two Waretown brothers married sisters, daughters of Captain Holmes. For a while, the Birdsall brothers lived across the street from each other in Waretown, until Amos built a bigger, fancier home in Toms River.

"The Cedars" may have been the home of Captain Holmes, or it could have been one of Waretown's many guest houses for tourists of the era.

When Waretown and Brookville split off from Union Township in 1876, we took the name "Township of Ocean," because our town's boundaries, like our sea captains, sail across the bay and through Barnegat Inlet.

By 1900, Waretown was a small town, but still a place of wealth and power. However, big changes loomed. The age of sail was over. Steamships driven by hard coal were revolutionizing seagoing commerce. Soon, ships too big and heavy for Barnegat Bay would become the primary means of water-borne trade.

The railroad, such a boon to the town, also changed how goods were transported, slowly sending the wealth and power of the coasting trade into the dusky veil of history.

Ever resilient, as the old coasting routes disappeared, our sea captains created a tourist boom for themselves: taking hunting and fishing parties out on Barnegat Bay. By doing this, they kept the glamour of sail alive for another quarter century, until it slowly faded away—like a glistening mist on a summer morning—and Waretown went to sleep. For nearly fifty years, we were the village that time forgot.

When I was a little girl in the nineteen sixties and seventies, Olga Smith was another one of my mother's great-aunts. In her nineties at the time, Olga remembered Waretown's glory days. She would shake her head and say, "Waretown was such a busy place then, so many people coming and going. There were ships at the dock and trains at the station . . . The town was bustling and alive. Now it is all gone, and it will never come back."

It made me sad to think there was something wonderful and exciting, something fine about living in Waretown that I had missed, simply by being born too late. Today, however, Waretown is waking up to upscale new housing projects and stores. The bustle is coming back, but in different ways.

Continuing our stroll through town, let's turn left from Jacob Howard Birdsall's gingerbread Victorian onto Pond Street on the map (today's Birdsall Street), for a glimpse at the home of his parents, Jacob and Rhoda Birdsall. Thankfully, this old home still stands, lovingly maintained by its present owners.

During the War of 1812, the British blockade was a serious impairment to the coasting trade. Commodore Thomas Hardy, in his 74-gun ship RAMILLES, was the commander of the British squadron off the Jersey shore. Jacob's father, Amos Birdsall, ran the blockade a

Merriman postcard of the Birdsall Homestead, Waretown, from a glass negative. This was the home of Jacob and Rhoda Brown Birdsall, the parents of Amos and Jacob Howard Birdsall. While the Birdsalls of Waretown were Quakers, and remained neutral during the American Revolution, Rhoda's grandfather was a well-known local veteran. The Birdsall's neutrality did not stop the British from confiscating at least one of their coasting vessels during the War of 1812. This house still stands, although the street in front is no longer named for Abraham Waier's millpond. Today the address is Birdsall Street.

Merriman postcard of Birdsall Bridge, Waretown, from a glass negative. This little bridge was located on a small dirt road that led to Abraham Waier's gristmill, the miller for whom Waretown was named, and then on towards the center of town. By the time these post-cards were photographed, the Birdsall family owned the site of Waier's former gristmill. The road and the bridge are both gone today, swallowed up by private property lines. All that remains are the broken concrete piers on Waretown Creek.

number of times in his schooner, PRESIDENT. The only time that made it into the history books was when he got caught.

Hardy immediately seized the vessel. Because of heavy seas, Captain Birdsall and his crew were forced to wait on board the *Ramilies* for a few days. Captain Birdsall watched helplessly as Hardy confiscated everything of value. The hardest part must have been when Hardy disabled the beautiful schooner by sawing off its masts, making it a barge to be towed away. At least our Waretown men escaped impressment into the Royal Navy. Eventually, they were allowed to board a passing fishing boat and go home.[19]

Amos had a large family. Three of his sons continued as Waretown mariners: Samuel, who became the first state senator to represent Ocean County; Ezekiel, as discussed earlier; and Jacob, who married Rhoda Brown and built Birdsall Homestead. Rhoda's grandfather served in the American Revolution with Waretown's local min-utemen, the Fifth Company of the Monmouth Militia. Today, Jacob and Rhoda's address is on Birdsall Street, in honor of the family. However, when Jacob and Rhoda lived here, it was called "Pond Street" after Abraham Waier's millpond.

After retiring from the sea, Jacob Birdsall helped to carve Ocean County from Monmouth in 1850. During the Civil War, he served in the New Jersey Assembly. He was a founder of Cedar Grove Cemetery in 1861. In 1873, he was appointed as a Lay Judge. His funeral in 1877 was so large that an extra train was run from Toms River to accommodate all the guests.[20]

A little dirt road once led from the Birdsall Home-stead to the train station. It appears on the Woolman map. The lane is not named, but the bridge is marked. Birdsall Bridge crossed Waretown Creek near the spot of Abraham Waier's gristmill. Both the bridge and the road are gone today. All that remains are portions of the concrete piers, overgrown with weeds.

Merriman postcard of Waretown train station from a glass negative. This station was built in 1895. Franklin Eayre, the stationmaster, stands out front. The New Jersey Southern Railroad arrived in Waretown in 1873, and the last train chugged through town in 1972. Thomas Ackerman saved the train station from the wrecking ball by moving it to his own property and converting it into a dwelling. Many people watched with excitement as he towed the old station down Wells Mills Road behind his steam tractor. The Waretown office of Crossroads Realty sits on the postcard spot today.

Following this forgotten trail across the bridge, we arrive at Waretown's train depot. The New Jersey Southern Railroad came through in 1873, after quite a bit of wrangling with Tuckerton Railroad over who would win the route.

The railroad brought many jobs to Waretown. We had a conductor, firemen and brakemen. We even had a trackwalker, Isaac Brown Sr. Every morning, Isaac got up at 3 a.m. and walked to Barnegat station. The morning train to New York waited there. Isaac lit a kerosene lantern, and slowly walked the middle of the track, swinging his lantern back and forth, looking for anything loose or broken. He walked ten miles to Forked River, and reported the status of the tracks. "If all was clear, the message was telegraphed to Barnegat. Only then could the train leave for New York City."[21]

Many people still recall the excitement of waiting for the train to come in, when the boarders arrived for the hotels and the postmaster picked up the brown leather mail bag. Freight came and went, including local blueberries, cranberries, and oysters.

Watching the train chug into the station was a guaranteed distraction for schoolchildren, since the Little Red Schoolhouse sat across the street. Could *you* pay attention to the teacher when a train squealed in?

On the train station postcard, we can just make out Franklin Eayre, the stationmaster.

According to Al Stokely, a local railroad historian, the last passenger train came through Waretown in 1953, and the last freight train in 1970. The very last train through town was a fan trip in 1972. To save the station from being torn down, Thomas Ackerman moved it off site, making it his private home. The station originally sat where Waretown's Crossroads Realty office is today. The Rail Trail runs behind it, a hiking trail that traces the route of the tracks.

The Little Red Schoolhouse is our next stop (see the following page). It was located diagonally from the tracks,

nestled on the Woolman map between Railroad Avenue and Church Street (today's Bryant Road and Chapel Street). By 1875, Waretown was big enough for a school that did not double as a church on Sunday. Once again, the civic-minded Birdsalls donated the land.

At first, the exterior was white clapboard, and all eight grades learned together in the one room. Wooden benches stood in rows on either side of a pot-bellied stove. Girls sat on one side, and boys on the other.[22]

One early teacher, Stokes Collins, arrived on horseback from Barnegat every morning. Another teacher brought her little dog to school with her, and he slept under the coal stove. But my favorite teacher story is Mrs. Penn. Every now and then she would forget her false teeth, and had to run home and get them![23]

In 1913, the building was extensively remodeled. The schoolroom was divided in half, making separate classes for grades one through four and five through eight. Desks were purchased. The belfry was replaced with a smaller tower, and the school received its famous coat of

(Top) Merriman postcard of Waretown's public school from a glass negative. Built in 1875, this little school educated Waretown's children for 83 years. After the town outgrew the building, the school board donated the property to the Waretown First Aid Squad. Unfortunately, there was no place to house the ambulance, so it was stored across the street at Waretown Fire House. In 1969, the old school was razed and replaced by a modern First Aid building. Today's Little Red Schoolhouse Museum, at Waretown Lake, is a faithful reproduction of the school, by community volunteers. Visit at 182 Wells Mills Road, Waretown.

(Bottom) Waretown teachers and students in front of their school, 1901. This is the earliest school photo possessed by the Historical Society. At the time it was taken, eight grades were housed in one room, with a pot-bellied stove separating the girls from the boys. In 1913, the building was remodeled. Two classrooms were created—one for grades one through four, and another for grades five through eight. Waretown Elementary School opened in 1958. The town is now a K-6 district, with grades 7–12 attending Southern Regional. Courtesy of the Waretown Historical Society.

red paint. A well was dug and a hand pump installed for drinking water.[24] The Little Red Schoolhouse educated Waretown's children for 83 years.

The oldest class photograph of the school, preserved by Waretown Historical Society, is dated 1901. Although not a postcard, it gives a glimpse of the living people who inhabited the postcard world. Mary Bareford Hussong, (third from right, bottom row) recalled what a treat it was to be asked by the teacher to go get drinking water in the days before the pump was set. The lucky kids with that job walked over to Abraham Waier's mill pond to dip the bucket, then took their sweet time coming back. Everybody shared that bucket of water, drinking from the same dipper.

Ida Wilkins Letts (far right, bottom row) remembered how each family took turns bringing wood for the pot-bellied stove. When it was your family's turn, you got to sit closest to the fire.

By the late 1950s, the town outgrew the Little Red Schoolhouse, forcing overflow classes to meet in the Methodist church parsonage, and at Barnegat school. In 1958, Waretown Elementary School opened its doors. The old school stood empty awhile, until 1966, when the board donated the abandoned building to Waretown's newly-formed first aid squad. It was inadequate for the long term, as there was no room for a garage to house the ambulance. In 1969, the old school was razed for a modern first aid headquarters. Today, Waretown's Little Red Schoolhouse Museum is a faithful reproduction built by volunteers for the Waretown Historical Society. We have the original school bell, desks, and blackboard.

Continuing our walk down Railroad Avenue on the Woolman map (today's Bryant Road), we meet Thomas Gray, Waretown's village blacksmith, whose shop was right next door. Lillian Lopez, Waretown's "Piney Lore" poet, wrote a poem about him:

Merriman postcard of Waretown's village blacksmith, from a glass negative. Thomas Gray, 1839–1922, was beloved by the entire community. His shop was next to the schoolhouse, and the children loved to visit him during recess on rainy days. He taught them riddles and word games, as well as stories of sailing ships coming and going from Waretown Harbor. He made rings for the girls from horseshoe nails, and taught the boys how to whistle a tune by blowing through the holes in horse shoes.

*Village Tom*

Everyone in Waretown was friend to Tommy Gray.
His blacksmith shop was where men met to pass the time of day.
They brought their horses to be shod, they brought gear for repair;
He made clamming tongs and fireplace irons and tools and tin cookware . . .

His shop stood near the schoolhouse—it was like a little barn;
Kids gathered on rainy days to hear him spin a sailing yarn.
Young fellers vied for ways to help him, and Tom taught them well;
Amusing little ones with riddles, and tricky ways to spell.

Little girls in town wore rings he'd bent from horseshoe nails;
And boys blew into horseshoe holes to imitate his wails . . .
Yes, Tom Gray was a handsome man in character and face;
His descendants can be proud he left his mark upon this place.[25]

Petty Motorworks auto repair is on the spot today.

We cannot leave early Waretown without a promenade to the end of Bay Street, today's Bryant Road, for a glimpse of Barnegat Bay. Notice the rock pile in the photograph below. During the age of sail, those rocks were used as ballast in the old coasting vessels. A ship empty of cargo was too light in the water, too easy to tip over in high seas. So, after unloading their cargo, the old captains filled the lower decks with big rocks, to keep the ship steady on the way home.

Back in Waretown, the rocks were removed to make room for more cargo on the next trip. Leftover ballast rocks were piled on the bay front. Some were used to make a jetty. Time and tides have scattered most of them, but you can still sometimes see the tops of the rocks by Waretown dock at low tide. The next time you do, remember sailing ship days, and Waretown's maritime history.

When "The Little Fishers" was taken, Waretown was in high-swing as a sportsman's paradise. *Kobbé's Jersey Coast and Pines,* a tourist guide from 1889, describes the scene:

Barnegat Bay is all sport. In summer, hundreds of little vessels scud over its waters to the fishing grounds near the inlet; and of the early mornings in winter, the figures of gunners may be seen dimly outlined against the gray horizon, as they row their sneak boxes out of the creeks toward some sedgy point or island . . . There is an amusing rivalry between the different places along the bay shore for pre-eminence as sporting headquarters, especially between Forked River, Waretown, and Barnegat . . . the reason lies in the fact that the best fishing-grounds and shooting points are in their vicinity . . . In point of fact, Waretown is the most favorably located of the three places for fishing excursions, because

Merriman postcard of "The Little Fishers," Waretown, from a glass negative. No record exists of who these children are. The jetty where they sit was located in Barnegat Bay at the end of today's Bryant Road. It was composed of ballast rocks from Waretown's old coasting vessels. Most of the rocks are scattered today, but a few can still sometimes be seen at low tide.

A photograph of Waretown Dock at the end of Bay Road (today's Bryant Road), taken at the same time period as the Merriman postcards. This photograph clearly shows the ballast rocks where the previous photograph was taken. Courtesy Waretown Historical Society.

there a tongue of solid ground penetrates the salt meadows to the edge of the bay, and the landing is within a few minutes of the railroad station.[26]

Although the the photograph above is not one of the postcards, it shows the dock at the end of Bryant Road during the height of Waretown's hunting and fishing lodge heyday. You can easily recognize the rock pile where "The Little Fishers" was taken.

Just behind the bayfront dock stood the Bayview Hotel. This postcard is a print of one of the missing glass negatives from the original set; one that must have been broken. The hotel did not sit directly on the bay front, as the picture seems to imply, but further back, on what is today county-owned land. The area directly in front of the hotel was an open meadow, where the Bayview Condominiums now sit.

Built by Jacob Howard Birdsall, The Bayview Hotel entertained High Society. Its grand opening was July 4, 1890. It had 50 guest rooms, a restaurant and a bar. It was equipped with "all the modern improvements."[27] Its elegant grand staircase ran from the upper floors to the lobby below. The Bayview was the jewel of Waretown's tourist industry.

Captain Birdsall spared no expense. He sent a car to the train station every afternoon to pick up his guests. He ordered all the meats for his restaurant delivered fresh daily on the New York train. The Bayview also took quite a bit of pride in the "shore dinners" served at their restaurant. They included locally caught fish, clams, scallops, and oysters, as well as game birds from our marshes.

Just to give you an idea of how important Waretown was back in the day, our Bayview Hotel, Atlantic House, and other guest houses welcomed many celebrities to our bay shore. Local lore recalls that our VIP guest list included Buffalo Bill Cody, President Grover Cleveland, President William McKinley, and Babe Ruth.[28]

The Bayview was used as a barracks for soldiers during World War II. According to Jack Baker of

Merriman postcard of the Bayview Hotel, Waretown. No glass negative exists. The Bayview Hotel was located at the end of today's Bryant Road, just behind the salt meadows at the bayfront. Courtesy of the Paul W. Schopp Collection.

Point Pleasant, most people had no idea how close the enemy actually was to the Jersey Shore. German subs prowled within twenty miles of our coast. Locals heard depth charges booming. Fishermen saw periscopes all the time.

The coast guard patrolled LBI beaches on horseback. Boats had to possess a pass to get through the inlet. The coast guard boarded all boats before allowing them to pass, making sure they were not bringing supplies out to the German subs.[29]

Several people have shared memories with me about the soldiers stationed at the Bayview. Their jeeps and trucks came and went, and they were often seen marching down our streets or standing guard on bay roads. The mosquitoes were so bad in the salt marshes back then, the soldiers had to wear mosquito netting over their faces for protection.

Kids watched military convoys rolling down the road to the hotel from the windows of the Little Red Schoolhouse. It was a nervous time, even for the children. When a siren went off, they all had to hide under their desks. For Waretown's young women, however, the soldiers' presence meant fun and excitement, as lively dances were held at the boat house across from the hotel on Saturday nights.

The soldiers were the last of the Bayview's year-round guests. After they moved on, the hotel was only used in the summer. As the 1950s progressed, hints of the Bayview's former glamour remained. A pianist named Big Tiny Little played there, who also regularly appeared on the Lawrence Welk television show. The Bayview settled down to a quieter life, less busy than in its glory days.

The end of the Bayview came quite suddenly. A terrible fire broke out on March 23, 1960, one of the worst in Waretown's history. Many people have vivid memories of watching in horror and amazement as the old landmark burned to the ground.

Besides the hotel, Jacob Howard Birdsall made another big investment in Waretown—He built a dam on Waretown Creek to create a cranberry bog.

The cranberry industry took off in Ocean County circa 1860. By 1900, thousands of acres of cedar swamp became cranberry bogs. Since they were fresh water, ice was also harvested in the days before refrigeration. Stored in icehouses with hay or sawdust for insulation, ice lasted most of the summer.

Birdsall's cranberry bog was located in the woods between Wells Mills Road (Railroad Avenue on the Woolman map) and today's Memorial Drive. Once a large, thriving operation, this low-lying area around Waretown Creek has reverted to its natural wetlands state. A few wooden posts remain in the creek bottom where the dam once stood, and the ghosts of drainage ditches march through the woods in straight lines. Wild cranberry vines endure in many places, surrounded by spongy beds of sphagnum moss.

In 1916, Jacob Howard Birdsall sold his bog to Arthur and Stogdon Corliss. He retired to Palm Beach, Florida, where he died in 1919.[30] The Corliss family owned several more working cranberry bogs in Waretown, including a large one on today's Wells Mills Road. They built that one themselves in 1925, clearing trees and cutting irrigation ditches with a horse and wagon. They also owned three smaller bogs off Route 532 called "The Morey Place."[31]

The LeRoy Corliss Family bought Jacob Howard Birdsall's house in

Merriman postcard of the yacht Nautliss, from a glass negative. Fred Bahr was a life-long Barnegat resident and boat builder. He frequently took hunting and fishing parties out on Barnegat Bay.

Merriman postcard of Birdsall dam, Waretown, from a glass negative. I am unsure of its location. There are two possibilities: It could have been built for Jacob Howard Birdsall's cranberry bog, which was located in the woods between Wells Mills Road and Memorial Drive. It could also be the last remains of Abraham Waier's mill dam on Waretown Creek, built to create the pond for his gristmill in 1739. At the time the postcard pictures were taken, the Birdsalls owned both properties. The white spot in the photograph is created by a piece of tape affixed to the glass at some former time; we are afraid removal will damage the negative.

1950. Interestingly, LeRoy was a son of Arthur Corliss. So once again, the owner of Waretown's cranberry bog owned the most beautiful house in town.

In the early 1960s, the Corlisses sold the house to the owners of the Skippers' Cove housing development. The developers assured the Corliss family that the beautiful old Victorian would be preserved as a clubhouse for residents.

It would have been wonderful if the developers had kept their word. Can you imagine what a lovely, one-of-a-kind Victorian landmark Skippers' Cove would have had? How attractive it would have been for the entire town? "Of all sad words of tongue or pen, the saddest are these . . ."

Today, Waretown's cranberry legacy lives on at the Waretown Lake. Around 1970, after the Wells Mills Road bog ceased functioning, Ruth Corliss generously donated the property as a recreation area. Our Little Red Schoolhouse Museum, a replica of the old school, was built on the lake property in 2004.

I will close with a quote from Dr. Newbury, the son and grandson of Waretown sea captains. In 1937, Newbury described the Waretown of his youth:

> The shoreline of the bay was far different than it now appears . . . Waretown Harbor was filled with two and three-masted schooners, bringing pine wood from the woods back of Waretown to New York . . . Looking up and down the Waretown road, we knew that every house we could see was that of an active or retired sea captain.
>
> There was Captain John Holmes, Captain Enoch Jones, then Captain Bill Burden. That house

up there with a cupola on top was Captain Jacob Birdsall's. Captain William Warren was across the street. Then there were Captain Elias Chambers, Captain Charley Bowker, Riz and Henry Horner.

All over seventy, most ninety or more. I've often said that Waretown, with about three hundred residents, has more nonagenarians than anywhere . . . Every one of them came from rich Yankee stock . . . they were big men who knew ships, knew the sea, and who stayed in Waretown . . . when the world left them behind.

As the age of speed came, there was only the coast guard and this business of taking out fishing parties left for them . . . I remember when the road out to the Harbor went out into what is now deep water. There was room for a four-mule team, with a load of wood and charcoal, to turn around. Now the three rock piles offshore recall the old road.[32]

The Waretown postcards open a window to the people and places that Newberry recalled, giving a glimpse of the age they lived in. We have felt their echoes in the many beautiful eighteenth- and nineteenth-century homes still to be found on or near Main Street, lovingly preserved by present owners. Their spirits linger in our oldest cemeteries, among their beautiful monuments and poignant epitaphs.

Here the glass negatives end, and our window on the past closes. Shall we put aside the time capsule, and return to the present? You can, but I want to stay in the sepia-toned Waretown of yesterday. I am turning back towards the Old Shore Road, and strolling home.

## ABOUT THE AUTHOR

Adele Sattler Shaw graduated from Rowan University with a degree in elementary education. She now attends Stockton University, studying for secondary certification in Language Arts. Adele is a life-long resident of Waretown, with family roots seven generations deep. In 1997, she helped re-start Waretown Historical Society, which had been dormant for twenty years. Adele now serves as president and historian. She presents programs all over Ocean County on Waretown's founding, history, and role in the American Revolution.

## ENDNOTES

1  H. C. Woolman, Theodore F. Rose, T. T. Price, *The Historical and Biographical Atlas of the New Jersey Coast* (Philadelphia: Woolman & Rose, 1878), 297.

2  John O. Beattie and Lillian Lopez, *Ocean Township, the Centennial* (Sun Printing, 1976), unpaginated.

3  Elaine Hoger, *Who's Who in Waretown*, compilation of family records (Waretown: Waretown Historical Society, 2018).

4  *Warren Family File* (Ocean County Historical Society: Strickler Research Library, 2010).

5  *Warren Family File.*

6  Bayard Kraft, *Under Barnegat's Beam* (Appleton, Parsons, & Co, 1960), 52.

7  Ibid, 51.

8  Ibid, 46.

9  Ibid, 51.

10  *New York Times*, May 14, 1884. *Stackhouse/Camburn Family File* (Ocean County Historical Society: Strickler Research Library, 2010).

11  "Thomas Stackhouse Obituary," *The New Jersey Courier* (Toms River, New Jersey), March 7, 1933.

12  *The Waretown United Methodist Church Consecration* (Waretown: Waretown United Methodist Church, 1968).

13  William Fischer, *Biographical Cyclopaedia of Ocean County* (Philadelphia: Smith & Co, 1899).

14  Corrine Mulbach, *The Birdsall Family* (Senior History Seminar, Lakewood: Georgian Court College, 1989), 4–5.

15  Pauline Miller, *Ocean County: Four Centuries in the Making* (Toms River: Ocean County Cultural & Heritage Commission, 2000), 395.

16  Mulbach, *The Birdsall Family*, 6.

17  Ibid, 5.

18  Ibid, 7.

19  Edwin Salter, *A History of Monmouth and Ocean Counties* (Bayonne: E. Gardner & Son, 1890), 291–92.

20  "Jacob Birdsall Obituary," *New Jersey Courier* (Toms River, New Jersey) September 27, 1877.

21  Billie Brown, "These Are the Things I Remember, Part II," *The Waretown Villager* (Waretown: Waretown Historical Society, 2001).

22  Beattie and Lopez, *Ocean Township, the Centennial.*

23  *Interview with Gladys Britton* by Henry and Anne Gerken and Fay and Engle Sprague, transcribed by Rod Schmidt (Waretown: Waretown Historical Society, 2006).

24  Beattie and Lopez, *Ocean Township, the Centennial.*

25  Lillian Arnold Lopez, *Piney Lore* (Compiled and edited by Karen Lopez Bishop, 1993), 103.

26  Gustav Kobbé, *Kobbé's Jersey Coast and Pines* (Short Hills, New Jersey, 1889; Baltimore: Gateway Press, 1970), 64–66.

27  William Fischer, *Biographical Cyclopaedia of Ocean County* (Philadelphia: Smith & Co, 1899).

28  Pauline Miller, *Ocean County: Four Centuries in the Making* (Toms River: Ocean County Cultural & Heritage Commission, 2000), 397, 846.

29  Christine Menapace, "Interview with Jack Baker," *Jersey Shore Magazine: Ocean and Monmouth Counties* (Spring 2013): 39.

30  Mulbach, *The Birdsall Family*, 4–5.

31  Beattie and Lopez, *Ocean Township, the Centennial.*

32  Henry Carlton Beck, *More Forgotten Towns of Southern New Jersey* (New Brunswick: Rutgers University Press, 1963), 324–25.

# Who Was Alick Merriman?
## A South Jersey Real Photo Postcard Photographer

Paul W. Schopp

Joseph John and Emmeline Ellen Pictor Merriman welcomed the birth of their son, Alick, on October 14, 1873 while residing in Chippenham, Wiltshire, England. At the time of Alick's birth, Joseph was age 29 and his wife, Emmeline, was age 28. By 1891, the Merriman family lived at St. Pancreas, London, England. When Alick and his family emigrated to the United States is unknown.[1] Four years Alick's senior, brother Reginald arrived on March 15, 1889, but there is no indication that other members of the family were onboard the same ship, the S.S. BRITANNIC.[2] Arrival years on the various census enumerations for Alick range from 1884 to 1887 to 1890 to 1891 and a thorough search within immigration records has failed to identify him, the ship on which he arrived, or his arrival date. There is no doubt that he and his family were already in New Jersey before May 1893, based on an Essex County directory.[3] That directory lists Alick as a salesman residing at 268 High Street in Orange, New Jersey, along with his two brothers, Percy and Reginald, both men also working as salesmen, and

their father, Joseph J. Merriman, for whom no occupation is listed. Two years later, the family had moved to 7 North 21st Street in East Orange.[4] In April 1896, Joseph John Merriman died at the age of 52.[5] A year later, Alick, now age 23, wedded Evelyn Elizabeth Meredith, age 25, and the daughter of John and Caroline Meredith, in East Orange. [6]

In 1902, Alick was the proprietor of the Universal Supply Company, located at 4 Valley Street, and Alick resided at 180 Valley Street in South Orange.[7] Then three years hence, Alick and his wife, along with Frederick and Clara Ardrey, incorporated the South Orange Motor Car Company with full capitalization of $100,000, of which $1,000 had been received. The new business not only engaged in automobile sales, but also bicycles and operated at 108 Prospect Street.[8] It appears the company had proven unsuccessful by 1907, for in 1909, the State of New Jersey revoked its corporate charter for failing to file an annual report and paying its taxes during the preceding two years.[9]

Apparently looking to make a clean start, Alick and

An A. Merriman view of the drawbridge at First Landing in Barnegat on the mainland. Of special note is the large stack of salt hay and the hay press in front of the pile. A man stands on the press, while another with a pitchfork is standing in the stack, feeding the press.

Evelyn, along with Evelyn's parents, relocated to the Jerseyville section of Howell Township, Monmouth County, in the first half of 1909. He purchased the James McChesney home on Colts Neck Road. In the latter part of May 1909, he had contracted with carpenter Ed Fielder of Adelphia to build an addition to the house.[10] The 1910 federal decennial census records the household containing Alick, age 38; Evelyn E., age 36; their daughter, Irene C., age 10; John A. Meredith age 68; and Carolyn F., age 60. The enumerator noted Alick's occupation as "photographer" working from home.[11]

While Merriman's work as a photographer—and particularly as a view or real photo postcard producer—is known, it is unclear how long he continued in this line of work. An August 1910 squib notes "A. Merriman, our hustling photographer, has a rush of orders. At present he and his assistant are working nights to fill orders for postcards."[12] In December 1910, he placed a newspaper classified advertisement offering 25 assorted Christmas postcards for $0.20 postpaid.[13] Other newspaper advertisements suggest Alick began dealing in real estate by February 1911, specializing in buying and selling local farms as a representative of the Osgoodby Farm Agency of New York.[14] No further mention of his photography work could be found after the end of 1910.

By November 1915, Alick had leased 26 South Street in Freehold, where he sold and repaired automobile, bicycle, and motorcycle tires and had a vulcanizing plant.[15, 16] He finally purchased the store building in 1919,[17] but in 1921, he sold the business and entered into real estate sales full time, opening a real estate office in the Theater building at 40 South Street in Freehold.[18] He soon became a representative of the nationwide Strout real estate company.[19] In March 1919, Alick acquired the L. Lawson Taylor property on Jackson Street in Freehold and moved his family in during April of that year.[20] Also in 1919, Alick received a patent for a new type of rubber cement he named "Kwikfix."[21]

He likely used this cement in his tire repair business. By 1925, the Merrimans resided in Manasquan. In September of that year, Evelyn purchased some property in Madison, Morris County, New Jersey.[22] The census enumerator for 1930 recorded Alick as owning a home worth $10,000 and he resided there with his wife and mother-in-law. His occupation is listed as "waterproofer," a business that likely grew out of his patent for the rubber cement.[23] By the time of the 1940 federal decennial census, Alick and Evelyn had returned to Monmouth County. Evelyn resided at 16 Potter Street in Manasquan, but Alick had entered the State Psychiatric Hospital in Marlboro.[24, 25] Alick died in the first half of 1943 and was interred in Greenwood Cemetery, Brielle, Monmouth County, New Jersey.[26] Evelyn survived him by five years before also meeting her demise. She is buried with her husband.[27]

Merriman did not stray from Monmouth and Ocean counties. In this view of Allentown Borough, Monmouth County, Alick has set up his camera on the south side of the mill pond and taken a photo of the Presbyterian Church and its burial ground.

## ENDNOTES

1 Ancestry.com, Reg Merriman family tree, Aleck Merriman Lifestory, accessed July 25, 2019.

2 Ancestry.com, Reg Merriman family tree, Reginald Merriman Lifestory, accessed July 25, 2019.

3 *Baldwin's Directory of The Oranges and Townships of Essex County…* (Orange, NJ: J. H. Baldwin, 1892), 205.

4 Ibid., 1894, 225.

5 Findagrave.com website, accessed August 1, 2019.

6 Ancestry.com, Reg Merriman family tree, Aleck Merriman Facts, accessed July 25, 2019.

7 *Baldwin's*, 1902, 742.

8 "State Charters For These Corporations," *Trenton Times*, March 10, 1905, 9.

9 *Acts of the One Hundred and Thirty-Third Legislature of the State of New Jersey* (Paterson, NJ: The News Printing Company, 1909), 584.

10 "Jerseyville Improvements," *The Daily Register* (Red Bank, NJ), May 26, 1909, 5.

11 Thirteenth Decennial Census for Howell Township, Monmouth County, New Jersey. Microform edition, roll T624-900, Enumeration District 0076, Washington, D.C.: United States Census Bureau, 1910, 16A.

12 "Jerseyville," *The Freehold Transcript*, August 19, 1910, 6.

13 "Christmas Bargain!!" *The Freehold Transcript*, December 9, 1910, 7.

14 "Small Farm Wanted," *The Freehold Transcript*, February 24, 1911, 5.

15 "Figuring Tire Costs," *The Freehold Transcript*, November 19, 1915, 12.

16 "Freehold and Vicinity," *The Freehold Transcript*, June 9, 1916, 7.

17 "Town Notes," *The Monmouth Democrat*, June 26, 1919, 1.

18 "New Real Estate Business," *The Daily Register*, August 31, 1921, 10.

19 "Freehold and Vicinity," *The Freehold Transcript*, March 30, 1923, 5.

20 "Freehold," *The Monmouth Democrat*, March 20, 1919, 1.

21 "'Kwikfix' Rubber Cement," *The India Rubber World* 61, 5 (New York: The India Rubber Publishing Company, February 1920), 300.

22 "Madison Real Estate Transfers Are Recorded," *The Madison Eagle*, September 25, 1925, 5.

23 Fifteenth Decennial Census for Madison, Morris County, New Jersey. Microform edition, roll series T626, Enumeration District 0031, Washington, D.C.: United States Census Bureau, 1930, 8A.

24 Sixteenth Decennial Census for Manasquan, Monmouth County, New Jersey. Microform edition, roll T627-2367, Enumeration District 13-88, Washington, D.C.: United States Census Bureau, 1940, 16A.

25 Sixteenth Decennial Census for Marlboro, Monmouth County, New Jersey. Microform edition, roll T627-2367, Enumeration District 13-93, Washington, D.C.: United States Census Bureau, 1940, 17B.

26 Findagrave.com website, accessed August 1, 2019.

27 Ibid.

Merriman has provided a wonderful view of Barnegat Bay that shows both sloops and a larger two-masted fore-and-aft rigged coastal schooner riding at anchor or tied to moorings. In the foreground is a view of the type of meadowlands lining the bay in this area. All three photos, c.1910, and from the author's collection.

# Publications on Jewish Farming in South Jersey

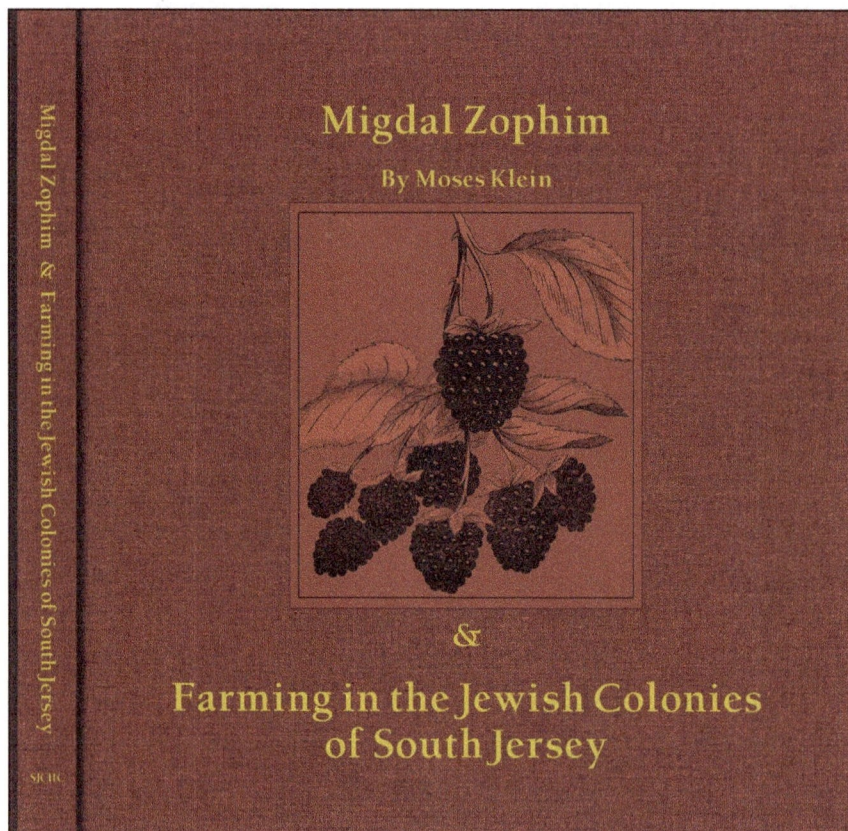

*Migdal Zophim & Farming in the Jewish Colonies of South Jersey* is published by Stockton's South Jersey Culture & History Center, 2019. This reissue of Moses Klein's 1889 description of the South Jersey Jewish colonies of Alliance, Rosenhayn, and Carmel, with additional contemporary news items, is accompanied by a scholarly apparatus. xxiv + 266 pages, paperback. ISBN: 978-1-9478898-9-7. $19.95

Our reissue of William Stainsby's *The Jewish Colonies of South Jersey* (1901) is a solid, brief introduction to Alliance, Rosenhayn, and Carmel and also Woodbine. 53 pages, paperback, ISBN: 978-1-947889-94-1. $9.95

Katharine Sabsovich's *Adventures in Idealism* (1922), the biography of H. L. Sabsovich, founder of the Woodbine Agricultural School, is forthcoming. These and other titles related to South Jersey Culture are readily available for purchase through Stockton, a limited but increasing number of South Jersey venues, and Amazon.com.

**The Alliance Heritage Center at Stockton University**

The Alliance Colony, founded a few miles northwest of Vineland in 1882, was the first successful Jewish agricultural community in America. Colonists had escaped the brutal pogroms of czarist Russia and, with the support of Jewish philanthropists, settled in South Jersey. The story of Alliance, from its roots to the present day, is an American story that resonates both nationally and internationally.

Stockton University and community partners seek to shine a bright spotlight on the Alliance Colony and related Jewish farming communities scattered across South Jersey, preserving, promoting, and disseminating their important history for future generations. To this end, the Alliance Heritage Center at Stockton has been founded during the summer of 2019 and has begun working with Stockton students and community members to document this intriguing aspect of New Jersey and American History.

# Shirley Burd Whealton
## In Memoriam (1934–2019)

I t's always sad to hear of the passing of a good friend and active member of our history-loving community. I lost both with the passing of Shirley Burd Whealton on July 30, 2019. She will be greatly missed.

Shirley was my "go-to" person whenever I had questions about the history and/or families of Tuckerton, Little Egg Harbor, and the surrounding Southern Ocean County area. She was unique in that she was able to seamlessly weave together knowledge of both the chronological and family history much as Leah Blackman did in earlier times. Her approach, however, was different. While Leah presented her information in a single book format which was common for the time, Shirley created a local history library as she collected, filed, and stored information in a variety of formats that others could use in their history and genealogy research. She willingly and liberally shared this information with all who were interested. I was one of these interested people.

Shirley was fascinated with local history since she was a little girl. Born in 1934, she grew up in West Tuckerton and graduated from Tuckerton High School in 1952. Her curiosity led her to talk with and ask questions of the Tuckerton "old-timers" who told her stories of Tuckerton in the late 1800s and early 1900s, invaluable information that was not readily available in history books.

This interest in local history continued throughout Shirley's life as she became active in a number of historical organizations. She was a founding member of the Tuckerton Historical Society and the Tuckerton Seaport Society and a member of the Tuckerton Old Home Society and The Great John Mathis Foundation. She is also remembered as being the first woman elected to the Tuckerton Boro Council.

Shirley married Charles Leslie "Les" Whealton in 1954 and settled down in Tuckerton to raise a family with 3 children—Keith, Kevin, and Karen. Even as a young wife and mother, Shirley continued her interest in local history. Often, after dropping her children off at school, she would walk through a local graveyard with pencil and paper, writing down the names and information inscribed on the tombstones and doing rubbings of some of the older tombstones. Eventually, she would type inventories of most graveyards in the lower southern Ocean County communities.

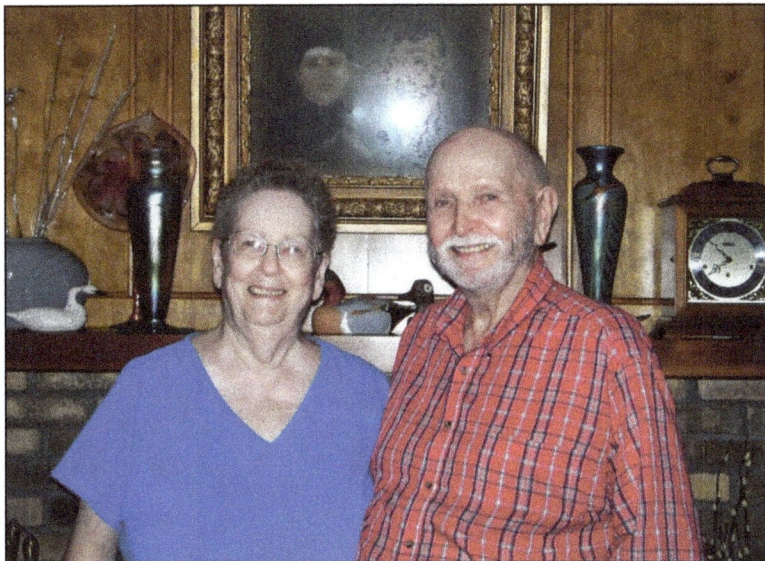

Shirley and Leslie Whealton's 60th Wedding Anniversary, 2013.

Les caught the history bug and would often accompany Shirley on her cemetery adventures and other history excursions. I am especially appreciative of their efforts as, more than once, these early cemetery inventories provided information that was no longer available as some tombstones have become unreadable due to weather degradation or vandalism.

Over the years, Shirley and Les travelled throughout southern Ocean County collecting a variety of historical and genealogical information from area churches, funeral homes, fraternal organizations, vital statistics from local towns and counties, and a wide variety of clippings from local newspapers which they often shared with local libraries and historical societies. I am forever grateful that their efforts have preserved a great deal of local history that might have been lost or become too difficult to access.

Their spare bedroom became the unofficial local area history library with the addition of bookshelves, filing cabinets, two desks, and a copy machine. Eventually, two computers were added to digitize the growing collection of data, providing more efficient access to their increasingly expanding collection of information.

The computers proved especially beneficial with the advent of genealogical software. Shirley worked diligently in entering information for over 29,000 persons into "Family Tree Maker" which allowed her to produce numerous genealogy reports encompassing most of the older families in Tuckerton, Little Egg Harbor, and surrounding southern Ocean County communities. The Whealton children, with the help of John Yates from the Tuckerton Historical Society, are in the process of working with the South Jersey Culture & History Center at Stockton University to make this invaluable genealogical database available to the public for research purposes. It would be a fitting tribute to Shirley's dedication to preserving Southern Ocean County history and genealogy. I am unaware of any other genealogy resource that can match its scope and detail.

I had the pleasure of working with Shirley on a genealogy project that was near and dear to her heart. She began clipping obituaries from local newspapers sometime in the early 1950s. She scrupulously mounted them on index cards that were alphabetically filed by the deceased name.

As technology advanced, Shirley enlisted me in assisting with the obituary project by scanning the obituaries from her notecards to searchable digital computer files. The collection was further enlarged when we were able to gain access to digital editions of *The Tuckerton Beacon* and the *N. J. Courier* newspapers. We had collected and organized over 10,000 searchable, digital obituaries from Barnegat south to New Gretna by the time of Shirley's passing. Hopefully, this collection will eventually be made available for research in the South Jersey Collections of Stockton University's Bjork Library.

My memories of Shirley are bittersweet. Sad, that I am no longer able to call her with questions about old-time Tuckerton or to work with her on a history or genealogy project and sweet, that I have a myriad of pleasant memories of happy times talking about and reliving local history with someone I had grown to love as well as to respect as a historian.

Peter H. Stemmer
August, 2019

**Thanksgiving Ox-Roast**. Ox roasts were a fairly common event during the nineteenth and into the early twentieth century, often serving as a fundraiser. A note on page 3 of the *Bridgeton Evening News'* Saturday, October 10, 1908 edition, announced the following: "The Holly Beach Yacht Club members are making preparations for the holding of a big ox roast on Thanksgiving day, the proceeds of which will be devoted to clearing off a mortgage on their club house." The image to the right ably demonstrates that the club members achieved their goal. Notice the size of the spit and the handle for turning the large ox carcass over the open flames. The ox roast took place at Ottens Harbor and photographer C. F. Saiber of Holly Beach (Wildwood) was on hand to capture the event.

# Call for Articles

The South Jersey Culture & History Center at Stockton University publishes twice yearly issues of *SoJourn*. We actively seek community members, avocational historians, and scholars to contribute essays on topics related to South Jersey. Illustrations to accompany these articles will be a plus. Articles should be written for laypersons who are interested and curious about South Jersey topics, but do not necessarily have expertise in the areas covered. Potential authors should check SJCHC's website for a link to a simplified style sheet guide for article preparation—www.stockton.edu/sjchc/—or just follow the style in this issue. Journal editors will be happy to guide any would-be authors. In certain instances, Stockton editing interns may be assigned to help research topics and/or assist authors with writing.

SAMPLE TOPICS MIGHT INCLUDE:

Biographical sketches of important but forgotten local people; the development or succession of a community's roads, bridges or buildings; local transportation (focused by mode, area or era) and what changes it wrought in the served communities; history of community businesses and industries (wineries, garment factories, agriculture, boat building, clamming, etc.); old school houses, old hotels, or meeting halls; narrative descriptions of local geographical features; essays concerned with folklore, music, arts; and reviews of new local interest publications. Photo essays and old photograph and postcard reproductions are welcome with applicable captions. In short, if a South Jersey topic interests you, it will likely interest *SoJourn*'s readers.

PARAMETERS FOR SUBMISSIONS:
• Submissions must pertain to topics bounded within the eight southernmost counties of New Jersey (Burlington & Ocean Counties and south)
• Manuscripts should be approximately 3,000–4,000 words long (5 to 7 pages of single-spaced text and 9 to 12 pages including images)
• Manuscripts should conform to the *SoJourn* style sheet, available here: https://blogs.stockton.edu/sjchc/sojourn-style-sheet/
• Manuscripts, if at all possible, should be submitted in digital format (Word- or pdf-formatted documents preferred)
• Images should be submitted as high-resolution tiff- or jpeg-formatted files (editors can assist with digital conversion of photos if necessary). 300 dpi resolution, or higher, preferred
• Complete and appropriate citations printed as endnotes should be employed (see style sheet). If using Word, please use its automated endnote function
• Original submissions only. Copyright licenses for all images must be obtained by the author or should be copyright-free figures and/or figures in the public domain
• If essays are accepted, authors should submit a short 50 to 100 word autobiographical statement
• Articles need to be more than just a chronology of the given topic. The author should be able to properly contextualize the subject by answering such questions as: a) why is this important?; b) what is the impact on the local or regional history? and c) how does it compare to similar events/personages/changes/processes in other localities?

CALL FOR SUBMISSIONS:

Submissions for winter issues are due before September 1; for summer issues, January 15.

Send inquiries or submissions to Thomas.Kinsella@stockton.edu or Paul.Schopp@stockton.edu.

The iron star used as section separator above, and at the conclusion of several articles, is part of a small collection of ironwork salvaged from the haybarn on the property of Buzby's general store in Chatsworth, New Jersey. The barn had fallen into disrepair and Marilyn Schmidt, who restored the Buzby property in 1999, had the structure disassembled. The cedar boards of the barn were repurposed to rebuild the Buzby outhouse in 2001. This ironwork is available for inspection in Special Collections, the Bjork Library, Stockton University.

www.ingramcontent.com/pod-product-compliance
Lightning Source LLC
Chambersburg PA
CBHW080524090426

42734CB00015B/3157